D1523009

Mental Illness

Other books in the Issues That Concern You series:

ISSUES THAT CONCERN YOU

Mental Illness

Lorraine Savage, *Book Editor*

GREENHAVEN PRESS
A part of Gale, Cengage Learning

GALE
CENGAGE Learning™

Detroit • New York • San Francisco • New Haven, Conn • Waterville, Maine • London

Christine Nasso, *Publisher*
Elizabeth Des Chenes, *Managing Editor*

© 2009 Greenhaven Press, a part of Gale, Cengage Learning

Gale and Greenhaven Press are registered trademarks used herein under license.

For more information, contact:
Greenhaven Press
27500 Drake Rd.
Farmington Hills, MI 48331-3535
Or you can visit our Internet site at http://gale.cengage.com

ALL RIGHTS RESERVED.
No part of this work covered by the copyright herein may be reproduced, transmitted, stored, or used in any form or by any means graphic, electronic, or mechanical,
including but not limited to photocopying, recording, scanning, digitizing, taping, Web
distribution, information networks, or information storage and retrieval systems, except
as permitted under Section 107 or 108 of the 1976 United States Copyright Act, without
the prior written permission of the publisher.

For product information and technology assistance, contact us at

Gale Customer Support, 1-800-877-4253
For permission to use material from this text or product, submit all requests online at
www.cengage.com/permissions

Further permissions questions can be emailed to permissionrequest@cengage.com

Articles in Greenhaven Press anthologies are often edited for length to meet page
requirements. In addition, original titles of these works are changed to clearly present the main thesis and to explicitly indicate the author's opinion. Every effort is made
to ensure that Greenhaven Press accurately reflects the original intent of the authors.
Every effort has been made to trace the owners of copyrighted material.

Cover image David Buffington/PhotoDisc/Getty Images

LIBRARY OF CONGRESS CATALOGING-IN-PUBLICATION DATA

Mental illness / Lorraine Savage, book editor.
   p. cm. — (Issues that concern you)
   Includes bibliographical references and index.
   ISBN 978-0-7377-4348-7 (hardcover)
1. Mental illness. 2. Psychology, Pathological. I. Savage, Lorraine.
   RC454.4.M462 2009
   616.89—dc22

                                          2008046781

Printed in the United States of America
1 2 3 4 5 6 7 13 12 11 10 09

CONTENTS

It may surprise some to learn that in the United States, 25 percent of people have some form of mental illness. Four of the top ten leading causes of disability in the United States are bipolar disorders, depression, schizophrenia, and obsessive-compulsive disorders. Eight million Americans have depression; 2 million have schizophrenia. Mental illness is not just a problem for the United States. It is expected to be the second leading cause of death worldwide by 2020, according to the World Health Organization.

Causes of Mental Illness

Mental diseases may have biological causes, such as brain injury, lack of oxygen during an accident, chemical changes in the brain, or genetic factors. Some even say malnutrition can cause mental illness. Environment can also cause mental illness, such as a childhood filled with violence and sexual abuse, a traumatic event like a divorce or death in the family, a natural disaster like Hurricane Katrina, or alcohol and drug abuse.

Diagnosis of Mental Illness Is Increasing

One of the reasons for the increase in rates of mental illness is better diagnosis. For years, mental illness has retained a stigma. People were reluctant to show signs of mental weakness or to even visit a doctor if they thought they had a mental health issue. Today, because there is less of a stigma, and more people visit the doctor for treatment, better diagnoses can pinpoint problems. More people are diagnosed and treated for common mental illnesses, such as depression, anxiety, and bipolar disorder.

To improve the diagnosis of mental illness, the American Psychiatric Association in 2000 presented the revised and updated *Diagnostic and Statistical Manual of Mental Disorders*, Fourth Edition, Text Revision (*DSM-IV-TR*). Used by physicians and psychiatrists for both child and adult patients, the *DSM* provides

Twenty-five percent of Americans have some form of mental illness.

a checklist of symptoms and causes of a variety of mental disorders. With the improved *DSM* manual, mental health professionals are recognizing, diagnosing, and treating severe illnesses such as depression and bipolar disorder much earlier in patients.

Better Diagnostic Techniques

Although no laboratory test can detect a mental illness, exciting new areas of diagnostic developments today can identify mental illness and find new treatments. Scientists are learning to analyze genetics and biomarkers (such as genes, proteins, blood, and spinal fluids) to find a correlation between specific erratic behavior or hallucination and a specific mental disease, such as schizophrenia, bipolar disorder, Alzheimer's disease, or depression. Some companies are marketing home genetic testing kits to test for mental illness. These are unreliable, and people should always consult a doctor.

In addition, advancements in magnetic resonance imaging (MRI) and positron emission tomography (PET) scans allow scientists to detect neurological causes of mental disease.

Better Treatment for Mental Illness

In addition to improved diagnostic tools, new and improved psychotherapeutic medications relieve the symptoms of mental disorders to help the patient function normally and enjoy a high quality of life. Research in the areas of selective serotonin reuptake inhibitors (SSRIs) created the best-selling drugs Prozac, Paxil, and Zoloft for depression. Advances in antipsychotic medication include clozapine (brand name Clozaril), which has been shown to be more effective than chlorpromazine (Thorazine) in patients with early stage schizophrenia. In addition to lithium, which has been around since the 1950s, new treatments for bipolar disorder include divalproex sodium (brand name Depakote), an anticonvulsant used to control manic episodes.

Overdiagnosis of Mental Illness?

While medical advances are surely beneficial for diagnosing and treating sick people, some in the medical and lay communities are crying foul. Allan V. Horwitz and Jerome C. Wakefield, authors of *The Loss of Sadness: How Psychiatry Transformed Normal Sorrow into Depressive Disorder*, contend that our culture is conditioned to find a medical reason for every problem. They say that doctors are being pressured by pharmaceutical companies to label every sadness, shyness, or fatigue a mental disorder. If you have a "mental disorder," then you need a pill to fix it.

An April 2007 study in the *Archives of General Psychiatry* reported that 25 percent of people who receive a diagnosis of clinical depression are actually feeling normal sadness, loss, and anxiety common to everyone who has experienced a traumatic life event, such as a divorce, natural disaster, death in the family, or loss of a job.

The growing rate of incidence of mental illness has many causes. *Issues That Concern You: Mental Illness* explores these causes.

In addition, the volume includes a bibliography, a list of organizations to contact for further information, and other useful appendixes. The appendix titled "What You Should Know About Mental Illness" offers vital facts about mental illness and how it affects young people. The appendix "What You Should Do About Mental Illness" discusses various solutions to the problems of mental illness. These many useful features make *Issues That Concern You: Mental Illness* a valuable resource. Given the growing social and medical costs of mental illness to society, having a greater understanding of this issue is critical.

ONE

Facts About the Most Common Mental Illnesses

Substance Abuse and Mental Health Services Administration

As part of the U.S. Department of Health and Human Services, the Substance Abuse and Mental Health Services Administration (SAMHSA) Center for Mental Health Services provides information about mental illness and services for people in need. The following viewpoint, presented by SAMHSA as a booklet, explains that while everyone has mood swings, feels distressed, or has changes in concentration at one point in time, mental illness develops when these conditions become severe and debilitating. The authors of the following viewpoint offer the facts about the most common mental health problems and try to dispel some of the myths about anxiety disorders, depressive disorders, eating disorders, and schizophrenia.

Mental health problems are health conditions involving changes in thinking, mood, and/or behavior, and they are associated with distress or impaired functioning. When they are more severe, they are called mental illnesses. These include anxiety disorders, attention-deficit/hyperactivity disorder, depressive and other mood disorders, eating disorders, schizophrenia, and others. When these occur in children under 18, they are referred to as serious emotional disturbances (SEDs). . . .

"Myths & Facts: The Facts," Substance Abuse and Mental Health Services Administration. www.samhsa.gov.

Anxiety Disorders

Panic Disorder

Panic disorder affects about 2.4 million adult Americans and is twice as common in women as in men. A panic attack is a feeling of sudden terror that often occurs with a pounding heart, sweating, nausea, chest pain or smothering sensations, and feelings of

Mental health problems often involve changes in thinking, mood swings, and strange behavior, and they are associated with distress and impaired functioning.

faintness or dizziness. Panic disorder frequently occurs in addition to other serious conditions like depression, drug abuse, or alcoholism. If left untreated, it may lead to a pattern of avoidance of places or situations where panic attacks have occurred. In about a third of cases, the threat of a panic attack becomes so overwhelming that a person may become isolated or housebound—a condition known as agoraphobia. Panic disorder is one of the most treatable of the anxiety disorders through medications or psychotherapy. Early treatment of panic disorder can help prevent agoraphobia.

Obsessive-Compulsive Disorder (OCD)

OCD affects about 3.3 million adult Americans, and occurs equally in men and women. It usually appears in childhood. Persons with OCD suffer from persistent and unwelcome anxious thoughts, and the result is the need to perform rituals to maintain control. For instance, a person obsessed with germs or dirt may wash his hands constantly. Feelings of doubt can make another person check on things repeatedly. Others may touch or count things or see repeated images that disturb them. These thoughts are called obsessions, and the rituals that are performed to try to prevent or get rid of them are called compulsions. Severe OCD can consume so much of a person's time and concentration that it interferes with daily life. OCD responds to treatment with medications or psychotherapy.

Post-Traumatic Stress Disorder (PTSD)

PTSD affects about 5.2 million adult Americans, but women are more likely than men to develop it. PTSD occurs after an individual experiences a terrifying event such as an accident, an attack, military combat, or a natural disaster. With PTSD, individuals relive their trauma through nightmares or disturbing thoughts throughout the day that may make them feel detached, numb, irritable, or more aggressive. Ordinary events can begin to cause flashbacks or terrifying thoughts. Some people recover a few months after the event, but other people will suffer lasting or chronic PTSD. People with PTSD can be helped by medications and psychotherapy.

Generalized Anxiety Disorder (GAD)

GAD affects about 4 million adult Americans and twice as many women as men. GAD is more than day-to-day anxiety. It fills an individual with an overwhelming sense of worry and tension. A person with GAD might always expect disaster to occur or worry a lot about health, money, family, or work. These worries may bring physical symptoms, especially fatigue, headaches, muscle tension, muscle aches, trouble swallowing, trembling, twitching, irritability, sweating, and hot flashes. People with GAD may feel lightheaded, out of breath, or nauseous, or might have to go to the bathroom often. When people have mild GAD, they may be able to function normally in social settings or on the job. If GAD is severe, however, it can be very debilitating. GAD is commonly treated with medications.

Social Anxiety Disorder

Social phobia affects about 5.3 million adult Americans. Women and men are equally likely to develop social phobia, which is characterized by an intense feeling of anxiety and dread about social situations. These individuals suffer a persistent fear of being watched and judged by others and being humiliated or embarrassed by their own actions. Social phobia can be limited to only one type of situation—fear of speaking in formal or informal situations, eating, drinking, or writing in front of others—or a person may experience symptoms any time they are around people. It may even keep people from going to work or school on some days, as physical symptoms such as blushing, profuse sweating, trembling, nausea, and difficulty talking often accompany the intense anxiety. Social phobia can be treated successfully with medications or psychotherapy.

Attention-Deficit/Hyperactivity Disorder (ADHD)

ADHD affects as many as 2 million American children and is a diagnosis applied to children and adults who consistently display certain characteristic behaviors over a period of time. The most common behaviors fall into three categories: inattention, hyperactivity, and impulsivity. People who are inattentive have a hard time keeping their mind on any one thing and may get bored

Mental Disorders in Women, Men, and Children

Mental Disorder	AFFECTS		
	Women	Men	Children
Panic attacks	twice as many women		
Obsessive-compulsive disorder	✓	✓	
Post-traumatic stress disorder	majority women		
Generalized anxiety disorder	twice as many women		
Social anxiety disorder	✓	✓	
Attention-deficit/ Hyperactivity disorder		✓	majority children
Schizophrenia	majority women		
Bulimia nervosa	majority women		

with a task after only a few minutes. People who are hyperactive always seem to be in motion. They can't sit still and may dash around or talk incessantly. People who are overly impulsive seem unable to curb their immediate reactions or think before they act. Not everyone who is overly hyperactive, inattentive, or impulsive has an attention disorder. While the cause of ADHD is unknown, in the last decade, scientists have learned much about the course of the disorder and are now able to identify and treat children, adolescents, and adults who have it. A variety of medications, behavior-changing therapies, and educational options are already available to help people with ADHD focus their attention, build self-esteem, and function in new ways.

Depressive Disorders

About 18.8 million American adults experience a depressive illness that involves the body, mood, and thoughts. Depression affects the way a person eats and sleeps, the way one feels about oneself, and the way one thinks about things. People with a depressive illness cannot just "pull themselves together" and get better. Without treatment, symptoms can last for weeks, months, or years. Depression can occur in three forms:

Major Depressive Disorder

Major depressive disorder involves a pervading sense of sadness and/or loss of interest or pleasure in most activities that interferes with the ability to work, study, sleep, eat, and enjoy once pleasurable activities. This is a severe condition that can impact a person's thoughts, sense of self-worth, sleep, appetite, energy, and concentration. The condition can occur as a single debilitating episode or as recurring episodes.

Dysthymia

Dysthymia involves a chronic disturbance of mood in which an individual often feels little satisfaction with activities of life most of the time. Many people with dysthymia also experience major depressive episodes in their lives leading to a recurrent depressive disorder. The average length of an episode of dysthymia is about four years.

Bipolar Disorder

Bipolar disorder, or manic-depressive illness, is a type of mood disorder characterized by recurrent episodes of highs (mania) and lows (depression) in mood. These episodes involve extreme changes in mood, energy, and behavior. Manic symptoms include extreme irritable or elevated mood; a very inflated sense of self-importance, risk behaviors, distractibility, increased energy, and a decreased need for sleep.

The most important thing to do for people with depression is to help them get an appropriate diagnosis and treatment. Treatment, usually in the form of medication or psychotherapy, can help people who suffer from depression.

Do not ignore remarks about suicide. *If someone tells you they are thinking about suicide, you should take their distress seriously, listen and help them get to a professional for evaluation and treatment. If someone is in immediate danger of harming himself or herself, do not leave the person alone. Take emergency steps to get help, such as calling 911. You can also call The Hope Line Network at 1-800 SUICIDE (784-2433).*

Eating Disorders

Anorexia Nervosa

People with this disorder see themselves as overweight despite their actual body weight. With this disorder, [people] work to maintain a weight lower than normal for their age and height. This is accompanied by an intense fear of weight gain or looking fat. At times, [people] can even deny the seriousness of their low body weight. Eating becomes an obsession and habits develop, such as avoiding meals, picking out a few foods and eating these in small quantities, or carefully weighing and portioning food. People with anorexia may repeatedly check their body weight, and many engage in other techniques to control their weight, like compulsive exercise or purging by vomiting or using laxatives. Some people fully recover after a single episode; some have a pattern of weight gain and relapse; and others experience a deteriorating course of illness over many years.

Bulimia Nervosa

Bulimia is characterized by episodes of binge eating—eating an excessive amount of food at once with a sense of lack of control over eating during the episode—followed by behavior in order to prevent weight gain, such as self-induced purging by vomiting or misuse of laxatives, diuretics, enemas, or other medications; fasting; or excessive exercise. Because purging or other compensatory behavior follows the binge-eating episodes, people with bulimia usually weigh within the normal range for their age and height. However, like individuals with anorexia, they may fear gaining weight, desire to lose weight, and feel dissatisfied with their bodies. People with bulimia often perform the behaviors in secrecy, feeling disgusted and ashamed when they binge, yet relieved once they purge.

Schizophrenia

More than 2 million Americans a year experience this disorder. It is equally common in men and women. Schizophrenia tends to appear earlier in men than in women, showing up [in men] in their late teens or early 20s as compared to their 20s or early 30s in women. Schizophrenia often begins with an episode of psychotic symptoms like hearing voices or believing that others are trying to control or harm you. The delusions—thoughts that are fragmented, bizarre, and have no basis in reality—may occur along with hallucinations and disorganized speech and behavior, leaving the individual frightened, anxious, and confused. There is no known single cause of schizophrenia. Treatment may include medications and psychosocial support like psychotherapy, self-help groups, and rehabilitation.

TWO

Many Factors Cause Mental Illness

George Stewart

Mind is a mental health charity in England and Wales that provides information on mental health and promotes the needs and champions the equality of people with mental health issues. In this viewpoint Mind writer George Stewart describes the various causes of mental illness, such as family background, stress, biochemistry, and genetics. Even though doctors and mental health professionals debate these causes, they all agree that mental illness is likely caused by a combination of life experiences and genetic makeup. Stewart notes that although mental illness is common, it is among the least understood conditions in society, a situation that leads to prejudice and discrimination toward people with mental conditions. Nevertheless, he contends, people with mental illness can lead productive lives if they are properly treated.

Mental illness is very common. . . . There is a great deal of controversy about what it is, what causes it, and how people can be helped to recover. People with a mental illness can experience problems in the way they think, feel or behave. This can significantly affect their relationships, their work, and their

George Stewart, *Understanding Mental Illness*. Revised edition. London: Mind, 2007. www.mind. org.uk. Copyright © Mind 2007, reprinted from *Understanding Mental Illness* by permission of Mind (National Association for Mental Health). Reproduced by permission.

quality of life. Having a mental illness is difficult, not only for the person concerned, but also for their family and friends.

Mental illnesses are some of the least understood conditions in society. Because of this, many people face prejudice and discrimination in their everyday lives. However, unlike the images often found in books, on television and in films, most people can lead productive and fulfilling lives with appropriate treatment and support. For some people, drugs and other medical treatments are helpful, but for others they are not. Medical treatment may only be a part of what helps recovery, and not necessarily the main part. It's important to remember that having a mental illness is not someone's fault, it's not a sign of weakness, and it's not something to be ashamed of.

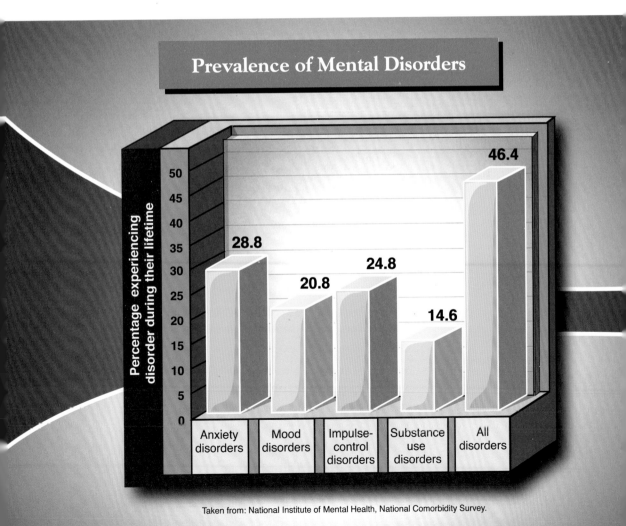

Taken from: National Institute of Mental Health, National Comorbidity Survey.

Seeing someone's problems solely as an illness that requires medical treatment is far too narrow a view. It discourages people from thinking about the many different influences on someone's life, thoughts, feeling and behaviour that can cause mental distress. It may also prevent people from exploring the various non-medical treatment options that are available. For these reasons, some people prefer to talk about mental or emotional distress, rather than mental illness.

How Is Mental Illness Diagnosed?

Psychiatrists have classified mental distress into different categories, or diagnoses. Making a diagnosis helps a doctor to assess what treatment is needed and to predict what is likely to happen. It can also be a relief to a distressed person to be able to put a name to what is wrong. But there are limits to diagnosis. Each person's experience of mental distress is unique and it can be misread, especially if there are cultural, social or religious differences between doctor and patient. Different doctors may give one person completely different diagnoses. Simply focusing on the symptoms can mean that not enough attention is paid to the person as a whole, and to their situation. Their experience may hold a meaning for them, which no medical diagnosis can do justice to.

If a diagnosis becomes a label, it can be very damaging. For example, instead of being seen as a parent, writer, mechanic or student who has schizophrenia, a person may be seen as 'a schizophrenic', as though this diagnosis summed them up. It's important to remember that a diagnosis does not have to determine the whole course of life, and may come to be a relatively minor part of an individual's identity or history.

It's possible to recover completely from mental distress and many do. Sometimes, they even emerge from the experience feeling stronger and wiser. Others get over the worst, but remain vulnerable, and relapse from time to time. Some don't recover, and will continue to receive treatment in the long term.

Psychiatrists aren't able to predict, accurately, what each individual outcome will be. Recovery is possible with all types of mental distress but, unfortunately, people are sometimes told that they won't recover. Such statements can become self-fulfilling because they add to existing feelings of hopelessness. It's important never to give up, whatever you are told.

What Forms Can Mental Distress Take?

Mental distress takes many forms. The terms used to diagnose them are sometimes words that are in everyday use, for example, 'depression' or 'anxiety'. This can make them seem easier to understand, but their familiarity can mean underestimating just how severe and incapacitating these conditions may be. Some of the most commonly diagnosed forms of mental distress are described below.

Depression

Depression lowers a person's mood, and can make them feel hopeless, worthless, unmotivated and exhausted. It can affect sleep, appetite and self-esteem, and interfere with daily activities. It may even affect their physical health. This may set off a vicious cycle, because the worse they feel, the more depressed they are likely to get. Depression often goes hand in hand with anxiety. . . .

Anxiety

Anxiety can mean constant and unrealistic worry about any aspect of daily life. It may cause restlessness, sleeping problems and possibly physical symptoms; for example, an increased heart beat, stomach upset, muscle tension or feeling shaky. Someone who is highly anxious may also develop related problems, such as panic attacks, a phobia or obsessive compulsive disorder. . . .

Panic Attacks

These are sudden, unexpected bouts of intense terror. A person experiencing an attack may find it hard to breathe, and feel their heart beating hard. They may have a choking sensation and a pain in the chest, begin to tremble or feel faint. It's easy to mistake these for the signs of a heart attack or another serious problem. Panic attacks can occur at any time, and this is what distinguishes them from a natural response to real danger.

Many people suffer panic attacks, which are unexpected bouts of extreme terror.

Having one panic attack doesn't necessarily mean that someone will have another one. But, sometimes, the experience is so frightening that people become afraid of having another. This fear may actually trigger another attack when a similar situation arises. . . .

Obsessive-Compulsive Disorder

Someone with an obsessive-compulsive disorder feels they have no control over certain thoughts or ideas that are highly disturbing to them, but which seem to force themselves into consciousness. These thoughts, or obsessions, create unbearable anxiety, which can only be relieved by performing a particular ritual to neutralise them. This could be something like repeatedly opening and closing a door, washing your hands, or counting. . . .

Phobias

A phobia is an unreasonable fear of a particular situation or object. It may cause major disruption to life because it imposes such restrictions on the way people live. Agoraphobia can cause such paralysing fear that a person may remain isolated in their own home, afraid to go out. Other common phobias include fear of animals, heights, flying and enclosed spaces. . . .

Bipolar Disorder (Manic Depression)

Bipolar disorder is a mood disorder. During 'manic' episodes, people tend to be hyperactive, uninhibited, reckless, full of grandiose schemes and scattered ideas. At other times, they may go through long periods of being very depressed. Not everyone experiences both these extremes. . . .

Schizophrenia

Schizophrenia is one of the most debilitating of all mental illnesses and can severely interfere with someone's ability to perform everyday tasks and activities. Symptoms may include hearing voices and seeing things that other people can't. Someone with these problems may become confused and withdrawn. . . .

What Are the Causes of Mental Distress?

There are many opinions about what causes mental distress. It's part of a wider debate about what makes people the way they are, whether their personality is shaped by the life experiences they have gone through, or whether it's determined by their genetic make-up, inherited from their parents. It's possible that some people are more vulnerable to mental health problems, which could be triggered by stressful or traumatic events. The following are some of the possible causes of mental distress. It may be due to any one of these factors, or to a combination of them.

Difficult Family Background

Growing up feeling uncared-for, scared of a parent, or having been sexually abused can make people highly insecure and more vulnerable to mental distress. But being much too overprotected as a child can also put you at risk.

Hidden Feelings

You may have been discouraged from expressing your feelings from a very early age. As a child, you may even have been pun-

Genetic links have been found in families with bipolar disorder, and parents with a history of the disease should have their child evaluated if signs of manic behavior are apparent.

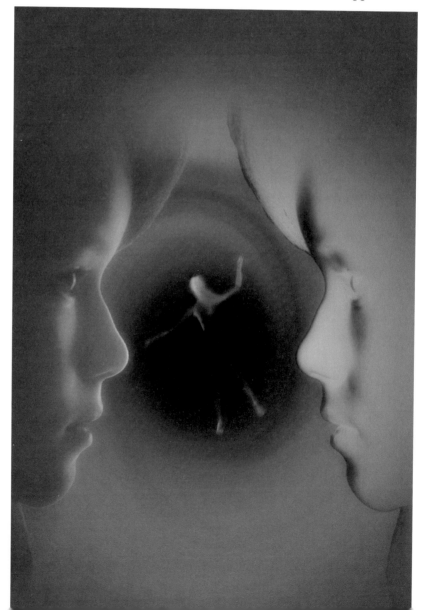

ished for getting angry, crying or laughing too loudly. Feelings that are held back, and which are not expressed, affect your physical and mental health.

Stressful Life Events

These may be traumatic events, such as the death of someone close, or longer-term struggles, such as being the victim of some form of harassment or oppression.

Biochemistry

Your body chemistry can affect your mind. For example, if you are frightened, it triggers the body's 'fight or flight' response to produce a hormone called adrenalin. If physical activity doesn't use up all the adrenalin, the body remains tense and the mind stays over-active.

Genes

You inherit physical characteristics from your parents and can pass them on in the same way. It's possible that your genes can also affect your personality. There are genes that cause physical illnesses, so there may be genes that predispose a person towards mental illness. There is some scientific evidence to support the idea that one person may be more likely than another to develop a particular problem, such as bipolar disorder or schizophrenia.

THREE

Genes Cause Mental Illness

Tina Hesman Saey

Science journalist Tina Hesman Saey writes for *Science News* on such topics as the brain, metabolism, HIV, and sleep deprivation. In the following article, she explains the latest scientific research that shows that genetic mutations and gene packaging contribute to the risk of a person's developing a mental illness. As a person develops, modifications in DNA and proteins influence how genes are squeezed into a cell. When defects occur in how the cells are programmed, they are damaged and mental illness can be one consequence. For example, when dramatic changes in DNA complex chromatin occur, a person is at risk of developing depression and addiction. In the future, new drugs will be able to program the genes correctly and prevent defects.

Genes' chemical clothes may underlie the biology behind mental illness. In research circles the debate is settled. Psychiatric illnesses are disorders rooted in biology.

As convincing as the evidence is, mysteries still fog our understanding of mental illnesses. Yes, the disorders stem from problems in the brain, but "on the other hand, for time and ages people have been looking at brains under the microscope, and they don't see

Tina Hesman Saey, "Epic Genetics," *Science News*, vol. 173, May 24, 2008. Copyright © 2008 Science Service, Inc. Republished with permission of Science Service, conveyed through Copyright Clearance Center, Inc.

much," says Schahram Akbarian, a psychiatrist and neuroscientist at the University of Massachusetts Medical School in Worcester. No lesions, malformations, scars or other outward signs distinguish a mentally ill brain from a healthy one.

Genetic Mutations Linked to Mental Illness

In recent years, researchers have searched the genome for mutations linked to mental illness. The scans have been fruitful, perhaps too fruitful. Hundreds of genes have been implicated in predisposing a person to such disorders as addiction, schizophrenia, bipolar disorder, depression or anxiety. But no gene has been shown to be a master switch.

The debate has raged for decades over whether mental illnesses sprout from nature or nurture. Scientists now suspect both. A new field linking genes and environment may chart the way for solving some of the mysteries shrouding mental illness.

Genes alone can only explain a few of the reasons people contract mental illnesses, become addicts or have developmental disorders, such as autism. Identical twins share a genetic makeup, so if genes controlled psychiatric disorders, whenever one twin developed a mental illness, the other would too. But that's not how it happens. Depending on the disorder, both twins develop it only about half the time. "We know the genetic risk of mental illness is about 50 percent, which leaves a whole other 50 percent unaccounted for," says Eric J. Nestler of the University of Texas Southwestern Medical Center at Dallas.

Genes Versus Environment

Some people say nurture, that is, "environment," is the root of psychiatric disorders, or at the very least accounts for the remainder of the risk. But no one has ever pinpointed exactly which experiences, infections, chemical exposures, types of stress or other environmental factors tip some brains into mental illness while others remain healthy despite the same insults, Akbarian says.

Scientists have also long sought explanations for why psychiatric disorders are so enduring, coming on slowly and then waxing and waning throughout life, or plunging addicts into craving, years after they've stopped taking drugs. Even the medications used to treat depression take weeks to grant relief.

The emerging field of epigenetics (which means "beyond genes") lies at this interface between genetics and environment and is revealing what marketers and Hollywood types have known for ages—that packaging is important.

Epigenetics is elucidating how environmental cues make their marks on genes. Such discoveries could help in understanding the mentally ill mind and lead to new treatments for psychiatric disorders and addiction.

Changing and Not Forgetting

Epigenetic mechanisms alter how cells use genes but don't change the DNA code in the genes themselves. The term "epigenetic" has been used for 60 years to describe the changes an organism experiences as it develops, but it has recently come to refer to the dozens of different modifications that DNA and its associated proteins undergo. All of the alterations essentially perform the same job: packaging genes properly.

Some of the modifications package genes so that they are shrink-wrapped tighter than a brand new CD, and just as hard to get into. Other epigenetic changes give cellular machinery easy access to genes. The ultimate effect is to finely tune to what degree a gene is turned on or off. Often the fine tuning is long-lasting, setting the level of a gene's activity for the lifetime of the cell.

Such extra-genetic programming is essential for cells to establish and maintain their identities throughout life.

"We don't need dopamine receptors in muscle cells, and we don't need neurons that produce liver enzymes," says Arturas Petronis, director of the Krembil Family Epigenetics Lab at the University of Toronto in Canada.

But the instructions for making dopamine receptors, liver enzymes, hair follicles and every structure in the body are found in every cell. Somehow unneeded genes must be shut down, and the genes that are necessary to form a particular cell type must be turned on. And once a cell's fate is determined, the course must be maintained.

Genes "without the right regulation can't perform all these functions," Petronis says.

Programming Cells

Enter epigenetics, the molecular equivalent of the permanent record.

Once cells are programmed to be a brain, liver or heart cell, "they remember how to be that cell for the rest of their lives," says J. David Sweatt of the University of Alabama at Birmingham.

When cells "forget" their epigenetic programming, cancer or other diseases may result. But sometimes holding on to a program can be just as harmful, especially if that programming spurs a craving for cocaine or leads to obsessive hand washing or endless depression.

Scientists are only beginning to learn how psychiatric disorders are linked to the packaging of DNA and the genes it contains.

One of the best studied of the epigenetic packaging choices is DNA methylation. Cells chemically mark genes they want to turn off by tacking a methyl group (one carbon and three hydrogen atoms) to the DNA base cytosine. But not just any old cytosine (the C of the DNA alphabet) gets modified. The alteration happens primarily where the DNA sequence consists mostly of C's and G's (the DNA base guanine). Scientists call such sequences CpG islands.

Link Between Genes and Mental Illness

Epigenetic Changes

- The packaging of DNA and its proteins
- DNA mutations
- Genetic programming errors

Psychiatric Disorders

- Increased susceptibility to depression, schizophrenia, addiction

Taken from: Tina Hesman Saey, "Epic Genetics," *Science News*, May 24, 2008.

Genes have control regions that work like light switches or thermostats to flip genes on or off or nudge the level of activity up or down. CpG islands are often found in or near these control regions.

When a methyl group is pasted onto a C, a sort of molecular police tape goes up, declaring a gene off-limits to proteins called transcription factors that turn genes on. Other proteins act as guards to make sure that no transcription factors sneak past the tape.

An illustration of DNA undergoing genetic engineering. Genetic material, RNA or DNA, may be introduced into a person's cells to fight or prevent mental disorders.

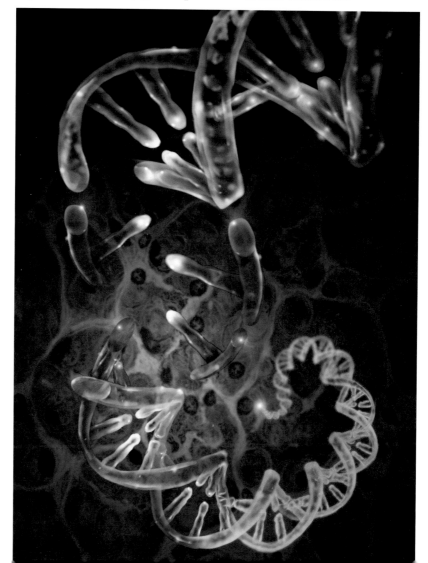

Programming Errors

Petronis and colleagues examined DNA-methylation patterns in brain tissue from deceased people who had had schizophrenia or bipolar disorder and from deceased people who had been mentally healthy. The group surveyed more than 7,000 CpG islands and found that about one in every 200 was methylated differently in people with major psychosis—a collective term for schizophrenia and bipolar disorder—than in people free from those disorders. That means that many genes are regulated differently in people with schizophrenia and bipolar disorder.

Some of the alterations affect activity of genes that are involved in regulating the brain's chemical communication system, its development or its response to stress. Some of the modifications even make tiny cellular powerhouses, called mitochondria, work differently.

Sperm from men with major psychosis also had altered DNA methylation compared with sperm from healthy men, the group reported in the March [2008] issue of the *American Journal of Human Genetics*. The result could mean that epigenetic packaging systems are faulty in people with schizophrenia and bipolar disorder.

"The good news is we have epigenetic changes," Akbarian says. "The bad news is that they are not so dramatic [as] to give the telltale sign of disease."

Several subtle epigenetic changes may add up to psychiatric disease, especially when paired with DNA mutations that make brains vulnerable to stress, he says.

Epigenetic Packaging

DNA methylation is only one of dozens of various epigenetic packaging materials. Epigenetics is all about "-ylation," that is, the addition of one kind of chemical group or another to various proteins, fats, DNA and other molecules. Adding an acetyl group to a protein, for instance, is called acetylation. Tacking on phosphorus is, yes, phosphorylation, and so on.

DNA and its associated proteins are known collectively as chromatin. The most intimate of those proteins—called histones—are popular targets for modification. To fit nearly six feet of

DNA inside a microscopic nucleus, a cell has to pack more efficiently than a tourist on a trip around the world. Histones are handy space-saving devices. Eight histone proteins get together and form a core around which DNA is wrapped. Other proteins help fold the DNA-histone complex into ever tighter structures until it can nestle comfortably in the cell nucleus.

These packing proteins are multitaskers. While stuffing DNA inside the nucleus, the proteins also help determine which genes will be turned off and on. The various epigenetic chemical modifications help direct the packing process, effectively deciding whether certain genes will be relegated to the bottom of the suitcase or stowed in accessible side compartments. . . .

Packaging Linked to Depression

Nestler and his colleagues have found that dramatic changes in chromatin packaging around a gene are linked to depression and addiction. Activity levels of a gene called BDNF (for brain-derived neurotrophic factor) in mice that are bullied day after day fall to about one-third the level found in non-stressed mice. The chronic bullying causes mice to avoid social contact with other animals, a symptom of depression. The "chronic defeat stress" experienced by the mice might also be a model for post-traumatic stress disorder, anxiety disorders and social phobias.

And just as people don't just snap out of depression, mice don't easily get over bullying once they are allowed to lead a peaceful life. Their defeated demeanors persist for weeks after the bullying stops, as does the reduced activity of BDNF in their brains.

Antidepressants, such as imipramine and Prozac, reverse the effects of bullying on both social interactions and gene activity, but only when the mice keep taking the drug. A single dose of antidepressants doesn't help, Nestler says.

That trend is similar to the way antidepressants work in people. The drugs typically take several weeks to change how people feel and usually must be taken long-term to maintain beneficial effects.

Nestler and his colleagues looked closely at what happens to chromatin around the switches that control BDNF levels. The researchers found stressed mice had much higher levels of histone methylation than non-stressed mice had. In this case, methylation helps to close off chromatin and adjusts the thermostat to turn down BDNF activity.

Imipramine restores gene activity in the stressed mice, but it doesn't remove the repressive methylation from the histones. Instead, it doubles acetylation of one of the histones. Acetylation helps loosen chromatin, allowing cellular machinery better access to the genes. The antidepressant didn't increase acetylation in unstressed mice, indicating that the modification only happens to genes that are already tattooed with methylation. The antidepressant may increase acetylation by inhibiting enzymes, called histone deacetylases, which would otherwise remove acetyl groups from histones.

In fact, the researchers found that bullied mice on imipramine made less of an enzyme called histone deacetylase 5 (HDAC5), but mice in the no-stress group had normal levels of HDAC5 even after taking the antidepressant. The finding is notable because antidepressants such as imipramine are generally thought to have no effect on healthy people but to lift the spirits of people with depression, the researchers said in a 2006 *Nature Neuroscience* article describing the study. . . .

Long-lasting effects of epigenetic packaging may seem to consign some people to a lifetime of mental illness, but scientists studying the disorders take heart that the problems can be influenced by packaging. That means that even people who have battled depression or schizophrenia for years may one day be able to take a medication that would repackage their genes in a healthier manner.

People who are susceptible to psychiatric disorders or addiction might be able to effectively inoculate themselves against the disorders by taking a tonic to prevent their genes from getting wrapped up incorrectly. Such [medicaton is] likely years or even decades away from showing up in the pharmacy, but scientists finally may be within yanking distance of the cloak of mystery covering mental illness.

FOUR

Omega-3 Fatty Acids Can Help Treat Mental Illness

Patrick Perry

Patrick Perry is a writer for *The Saturday Evening Post*. In the following article, Perry interviews Dr. Andrew Stoll and discusses the role of omega-3 fatty acids in reducing episodes for patients with bipolar disorder. According to the article, the typical American diet does not contain enough omega-3 fatty acids, which is one reason for the large increase in the rates of depression. This decrease in omega-3 fatty acids is a result of the shift from rural to urban life and the rise of fast food. In addition to Dr. Stoll's original study, further studies are finding that omega-3 fatty acids benefit patients with other mental illnesses, such as schizophrenia and ADHD.

Several years ago, Dr. Andrew Stoll, director of the Psychopharmacology Research Laboratory at Harvard Medical School–McLean Hospital, conducted a landmark study on the role of omega-3 fatty acids in bipolar disorder and came up with some surprising results. The researcher discovered that when patients with bipolar disorder consumed omega-3 from fish oil, they experienced a marked reduction in episodes of mania and depression. Extensive research continues to demonstrate that omega-3 fatty acids form the foundation of a solid, healthy diet, while also

Patrick Perry, "Battling the Blues: Ongoing Research Shows that Omega-3 Fatty Acids Help Treat Depression: An Interview with Andrew Stoll, M.D." *Saturday Evening Post*, vol. 277, May–June, 2005. © 2005 Saturday Evening Post Society. Reproduced by permission.

reducing the risk of heart disease, stroke, hypertension, and arthritis, among other conditions.

Omega-3 and Omega-6 Fatty Acids

Depletion of the essential omega-3 fatty acids in the typical American diet is linked to chronic disease and the huge increase in the rates of depression. Researchers now speculate that the increase in depression correlates well with the progressive depletion of omega-3s in our diet throughout the 20th century. The shift from rural community life to fast-paced urban sprawl also ushered in an era of fast foods, low fiber, and foods high in saturated fats, trans-fatty acids, and excessive intake of omega-6 fatty acids.

Omega-6 fatty acids are converted by the body into a number of strongly inflammatory hormones, collectively known as eicosanoids. Prostaglandins are the most well-known class of eicosanoids. If omega-6-derived eicosanoids are produced in excess

Nutrients in oily fish, such as salmon, may help prevent or relieve depression and bipolar disorder.

over time, the risk of developing heart disease, other inflammatory medical conditions, and, apparently, depression and bipolar disorder skyrockets.

The omega-3 fatty acid eicosapentaenoic acid (EPA) is converted into eicosanoids as well, competing directly with omega-6 fatty acids for access to the enzymes that convert these fatty acids into eicosanoids. Whichever acid wins the competition for these eicosanoid-producing enzymes depends solely on the ratio of omega-6 versus omega-3 consumption in the diet. This is crucial, because the omega-3-derived eicosanoids are largely anti-inflammatory hormones and have the role of keeping the omega-6-derived eicosanoids in check. Now, omega-6 fatty acids aren't bad, unless there is an excess over time.

Therefore, essential fats such as the omega-3s EPA and docosahexanaenoic acid (DHA) are necessary for optimal health.

Historically, scientists believe that our ancestors consumed close to a one-to-one dietary ratio of omega-3, found primarily in certain fish, to omega-6, commonly found in vegetable and seed oils. Today, researchers estimate that the ratio of omega-6 to omega-3 fatty acid consumption is somewhere between 20:1 and 50:1 in the United States, with an abundance of omega-6 over omega-3 fatty acids, which pushes us in a pro-inflammatory direction, more susceptible to heart disease, arthritis, and to illnesses related to inflammation, and perhaps depression and bipolar disorder.

Dr. Stoll's Research

To update readers about Dr. Stoll's ongoing research into the role of omega-3 fatty acids in depression, the *Post* spoke with the Harvard researcher and author.

Post: Do omega-3 fatty acids continue to demonstrate mood-stabilizing benefits?

Dr. Stoll: No one has replicated the findings of our original study as yet. The real story now is that there are now numerous positive studies on the benefits of omega-3 in unipolar depression, schizophrenia, borderline personality disorder, ADHD, and Huntington's disease. It seems that many disorders respond to omega-3s. Three of

Foods and Mental Illness

These nutrients and their food sources may help prevent or relieve mental illnesses, such as depression and bipolar disorder.

Omega-3 fatty acids
- oily fish—salmon, sardines, mackerel, trout
- eggs
- oils—flaxseed, canola, soybean
- nuts—walnuts, almonds, pecans

Folic acid
- dark green leafy vegetables—collard greens, kale
- broccoli, asparagus
- legumes—chickpeas, lentils, green peas
- papaya, strawberries

Selenium
- Brazil nuts
- tuna, cod
- beef
- poultry
- eggs
- rice

Tryptophan, an amino acid
- poultry
- soybeans
- cheese
- seeds
- eggs

Taken from: "Rise in Mental Illness Linked to Unhealthy Diets, Say Studies," *Natural News*, August 31, 2006. www.naturalnews.com.

the four studies in depression used EPA, or EPA plus DHA, and they worked. The fourth study used pure DHA—important for developing babies, pregnant women, and nursing mothers—and it failed. People hold onto stores of DHA for a long time, so you don't need to replenish levels as often as with EPA, which is turned over constantly, by conversion into eicosanoid hormones.

Post: Does EPA have anti-inflammatory properties?

Dr. Stoll: Exactly. The anti-inflammatory action of omega-3s has been definitively shown to help prevent heart attacks, in part by reducing atherosclerosis (hardening of the arteries). Omega-3s also appear to help cut down on the need for medications to treat rheumatoid arthritis, ulcerative colitis, Crohn's disease, and a number of other medical conditions. Omega-3s may also work in osteoarthritis. Research on omega-3s is exploding-and not just in psychiatry.

Post: Are you continuing your research into the relationship between fats and mental health, particularly omega-3 fish oils in bipolar disorder?

Dr. Stoll: Yes. We published the results of our first bipolar study, and the results were very promising. We went out on a limb to do this study with no funding and with colleagues sometimes ridiculing us. But the study was logical and rational, and patients, as well as informed and open-minded physicians, liked the approach. We tried it randomly and it worked. The same pathways are activated during bipolar disorder and depression, so EPA may perform the anti-inflammatory action.

Post: Do your patients, who were part of the original study, continue to take omega-3 and experience relief from their symptoms?

Dr. Stoll: I still see some of these people. All continue to take omega-3 supplements. In my practice, I am in favor of it, so I advise people to take it—if not for the psychiatric benefits, then for the general health benefits.

Side Effects?

Post: Is there a downside to supplementing with omega-3?

Dr. Stoll: There isn't. Some people may experience GI [gastrointestinal] distress if they take a large amount of a low-quality supplement. But the highest good-quality fish oil is not rancid and has little or no taste and has no side effects. Another issue that people worry about is bleeding, because EPA inhibits platelet aggregation. But we scoured the scientific literature, and there has never been a documented case of bleeding due to omega-3 fatty acids.

We recently reviewed about 18,000 people who participated in clinical trials with omega-3s, largely in cardiology studies, and we couldn't find one instance of bleeding in any of the trials. There was no bleeding, even if used in IVs prescribed before and during cardiac surgery. I think this perception is a myth because omega-3s don't inhibit the platelets as strongly as aspirin—perhaps 60 to 70 percent as much as aspirin—and unlike aspirin, the effect is reversible.

Finding the Optimal Dosage

Post: What dosage do you recommend for patients with bipolar and/or depression?

Dr. Stoll: Our omega-3-fatty-acids-in-bipolar study was the first controlled study in psychiatry. We really had no way of knowing what the minimum effective dosage was, so we decided to use a moderately high dosage that had been successfully used in omega-3 studies of rheumatoid arthritis and other medical disorders. This dosage was about 10 grams per day (6.5 grams of EPA and 3.5 grams of DHA daily). Most of the newer omega-3 studies in major depression used a very low dosage of pure EPA added to partially effective or noneffective antidepressants. For example, in one small study, Dr. Malcolm Peet and colleagues from England compared one gram a day of EPA to two grams a day of EPA, and up to four grams of EPA per day. One gram of EPA did the best by far. The most recent depression study, done by a group from Taiwan, was another unipolar study where they added omega-3 to an antidepressant regimen that was not working. They used the same exact formulation that we did—nearly 10 grams of EPA plus DHA in about a 3:2 ratio—with good results.

So, the question of optimal dosage remains unanswered. Practically, I start patients on one gram of EPA per day, and go up on the dosage gradually until an effect is seen on a person's mood. I usually do not have to exceed six grams of EPA per day. The amount of omega-3 in a supplement may be calculated from the side of the bottle.

Post: When consumers are looking at supplements, what is the ideal ratio of EPA to DHA that they should look for?

Dr. Stoll: This remains an unresolved issue, but I like a 7:1 ratio of EPA to DHA. That high ratio delivers plenty of EPA— the presumed active ingredient—and also provides an adequate amount of DHA. More DHA is required during pregnancy or while nursing to replenish stores. Most adults and children seem to have adequate or nearly adequate stores of DHA in their brains. Believe it or not, these DHA stores in the membranes of brain cells date back to a person's fetal life and [are] provided by their mothers. DHA turns over very slowly, so you don't need much to get by. In contrast, EPA is turned over very rapidly, as it is used for eicosanoid synthesis. For this reason, we think people are also much more depleted in EPA than DHA.

FIVE

Depression Is Underdiagnosed

David V. Sheehan

David V. Sheehan is professor of psychiatry and director of psychiatric research at the University of South Florida College of Medicine. He is a former assistant professor of psychiatry at Harvard Medical School and is the best-selling author of *The Anxiety Disease*. In the following article Sheehan explains that major depressive disorder (MDD) is underdiagnosed and undertreated due to patient non-compliance. Depression will strike about 35 million American adults, or more than 16 percent of the population, sometime during their lives. Primary care physicians must learn to recognize symptoms of depression, which may present physical and mental problems such as anxiety, substance abuse, heart disease, hypertension, and diabetes. Compounding the problem is that patients refuse drug therapy, due to side effects, costs, and the stigma attached to having depression. Physicians also need to improve follow-up with patients with in-office visits or telephone consults.

Major depressive disorder in the United States is a serious, recurring, and debilitating illness. More than 16 percent of the population, or approximately 35 million American adults, will suffer from it at some point during their lives. According to

David V. Sheehan, "Depression: Underdiagnosed, Undertreated, Underappreciated," *Managed Care / P&T Digest Depression*, vol. 13, June 2004. Copyright © 2004 MediMedia USA. Reproduced by permission.

the National Comorbidity Survey Replication, published [in 2003] in the *Journal of the American Medical Association* [JAMA] 12-month prevalence rates for major depressive disorder (MDD) translate to 6.6 percent of the population, or about 14 million U.S. adults.

To illustrate the magnitude of depression, consider this: In the United States, there were 30,622 suicides in 2001; most were by

More than 16 percent of the U.S. population will suffer from major depressive disorder at some point in their lives.

people with depression. By contrast, there were 20,308 homicides the same year.

Such widespread incidence and prevalence translates to a significant deterioration of quality of life, medical well-being, and personal productivity for millions of Americans. From a societal perspective, depression contributes to substantial worker absenteeism and disability and erodes billions from the U.S. economy. From a health plan or employer perspective, MDD is one of the most expensive disorders that payers face.

MDD is not simply the experience of a few "blue days." It is characterized by a severe persistent depressed mood and loss of interest or pleasure in normal activities. MDD commonly includes decreased energy, changes in sleep patterns and appetite, and feelings of guilt or hopelessness. To be classified as MDD, these symptoms must be present for at least 2 weeks, cause significant distress, and interfere with activities of daily living. If the depression is extremely severe, it may be accompanied by psychotic symptoms or by suicidal thoughts or behaviors.

Depression Underdiagnosed in Primary Care Setting

From all principal perspectives—the patient, the provider, and the payer—the problem is large and growing larger. This is due, to a great extent, to the fact that MDD is significantly underdiagnosed and undertreated—particularly in the primary care environment, where the preponderance of treatment for it takes place. Readers who are responsible for reining in ever-increasing pharmacy budgets may find this statement difficult to accept. With antidepressant drug use becoming more common among insured populations, their perspective has a certain validity.

For example, the medical literature documents a significant rise in the number and rate of outpatients being treated for depression over the past 25 years. In 1987, 0.73 per 100 persons were treated on an outpatient basis for depression; by 1997, that rate had increased to 2.33 per 100 persons—an increase of more than 300 percent (Olfson 2002). The same trend is documented with regard to antidepressant prescribing during office visits, with a near doubling of such visits over approximately the same time period.

So, while it is true that more patients are seeking help for depression and that utilization of antidepressants is on the rise, the question becomes: Is it adequate? The simple answer is no. Referring to the *JAMA* article cited earlier, it is clear that even with increased numbers of people now receiving pharmaceutical treatment for depression, this still only represents *just over half* of all patients diagnosed with the disease. Beyond that, of those who are receiving treatment, less than 42 percent receive adequate treatment. In short, less than 22 percent of all persons diagnosed with depression receive adequate treatment for their disease.

Comorbid Nature of Depression

There are numerous and complex reasons for this unfortunate situation. Rectifying it will involve patients, providers, payers, employers, accrediting agencies, and even governmental entities. We will touch on several of these reasons in turn.

Anyone involved with any aspect of the care of depressed patients must understand the recurrent and comorbid nature of the disease. The former serves to make an accurate diagnosis of depression more likely; the latter frequently contributes to missed diagnosis or misdiagnosis. Depression often is accompanied by other mental and physical comorbidities. These commonly include anxiety, substance abuse, heart disease, hypertension, diabetes, and chronic pain resulting from other conditions. Designing an appropriate treatment plan in the presence of comorbid conditions is understandably a challenge for providers, particularly when the depression is the underlying disorder.

Stigma is still stubbornly associated with depression and other mental illnesses. This must be addressed head-on with educational campaigns aimed at providers of health care, the public, and employers. The stigma of mental illness is a barrier to good care: When patients are unwilling or unable to share their symptoms with their health care providers, an accurate diagnosis and a targeted treatment plan will remain elusive.

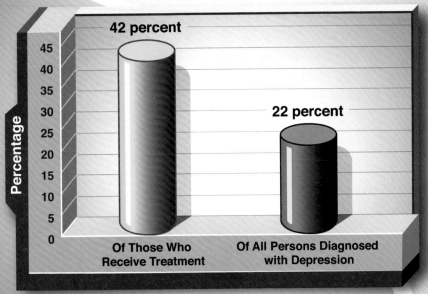

Those Who Receive Adequate Treatment for Depression

42 percent

22 percent

Percentage

45
40
35
30
25
20
15
10
5
0

Of Those Who Receive Treatment

Of All Persons Diagnosed with Depression

Taken from: David V. Sheehan, "Depression: Underdiagnosed, Undertreated, Underappreciated, *Managed Care Magazine*, June 2004.

Inadequate Follow-Up

Another obstacle to optimal care is lack of follow-up. This can result from physician time constraints, a weak link in the system that does not automatically schedule patients for an appropriate number of follow-up visits, or ignorance on the part of providers that in-office visits or even telephone consults can increase patient compliance and improve clinical outcomes. According to numerous studies, as well as anecdotal evidence, the well-informed patient will be a more compliant partner.

This lack of adequate follow-up is seen in the primary care setting as well as the specialist's office. It also has been the National Committee for Quality Assurance's point of entry. NCQA is an accrediting body with a mission to measure and improve the quality of health care in America. Using process measures as a proxy for quality, NCQA has developed numerous indices to evaluate quality of care. Several of these involve depression. Two of the measures concern adherence to medication regimens during the acute (12-week) and continuation (6-month) stages of the disease, and one measures the number of follow-up visits with a primary care practitioner or mental health care provider.

NCQA has established that 3 visits during the 12-week acute stage is the benchmark (1 visit must be with a prescribing practitioner). Yet, few health plans in America meet the benchmark; in 2002, across all plans reporting, only 19.2 percent of patients with a new episode of depression had at least 3 follow-up visits. Obviously, systems are not in place to guarantee that patients who are newly diagnosed with depression and prescribed medication are seen for what some would argue is a minimum necessary number of follow-up visits.

Noncompliance with Therapy

Besides lack of follow-up, dropout or noncompliance with therapy is a major documented problem. . . . Researchers found a 52 percent dropout rate by week 12 among a group of Medicaid patients who were prescribed antidepressants; only 27 percent remained on an adequate, 6-month course of therapy. Again, several causative factors can be identified. One is side effects; treatment-emergent nausea is the most common. Yet, if patients are made aware that this potential side effect is essentially gone within the first 12 weeks of therapy, compliance rates may improve.

Another causative factor in dropout can be a perceived lack of efficacy or unreasonable expectations regarding the length of time needed for the antidepressant to do its work. Again, good patient-provider communication is critical if patients are to have a realistic picture of what to expect from therapy. Unfortunately, a disconnect is evident in the respective perceptions of providers and patients about the quality of their communications. Providers assume that they have imparted more and better information about the therapeutic regimen than patients claim to have heard.

Yet another factor that may limit a patient's compliance is the cost of antidepressant medications. Employers and other payers are wise to give serious consideration to health plans and insurance policies that provide their employees, retirees, and dependents with adequate medication coverage that makes treatment affordable. Poor clinical outcomes resulting from lack of adherence to a therapeutic regimen are avoidable, and the downstream costs of follow-up care are potentially much higher than the cost of the medication itself. The most scientifically robust, evidence-based treatment algorithm will have little or no beneficial effect if patients cannot or do not follow their medication protocols.

So, the challenges are many and multifaceted. They involve people, organizations, policy, and process. Changing our nation's poor performance in caring for persons with major depression begins with awareness of these problems. Awareness leads the problem-solver to seek information and answers.

SIX

Depression Is Overdiagnosed

Allan V. Horwitz and Jerome C. Wakefield

Allan V. Horwitz is professor of sociology and dean of social and behavioral sciences at Rutgers University and author of *The Social Control of Mental Illness*, *The Logic of Social Control*, and *Creating Mental Illness*. Jerome C. Wakefield is professor of social work at New York University and has taught at the University of Chicago, Columbia University, and Rutgers University. In this article Horwitz and Wakefield discuss how depression has evolved from a simple feeling of sadness after a traumatic event to a clinical illness. The number of diagnoses of depression, number of patients being treated for depression, number of prescriptions being written for depression, and even the amount of media coverage of depression have all undergone staggering growth in the past twenty to thirty years. In the past, normal sadness was a condition characterized "with cause," for example the loss of a job or romantic relationship. It carried symptoms of insomnia, lack of appetite, social withdrawal, and lack of interest in everyday activities. Clinical depression was "without cause," the patient experienced no traumatic trigger event. But today, the diagnostic definition of depressive disorder, as listed in

Allan V. Horwitz and Jerome C. Wakefield, *Loss of Sadness: How Psychiatry Transformed Normal Sorrow into Depressive Disorder.* Oxford, United Kingdom: Oxford University Press, 2007. Copyright © 2007 by Allan V. Horwitz and Jerome C. Wakefield. All rights reserved. Reproduced by permission of Oxford University Press.

the *Diagnostic and Statistical Manual (DSM)*, includes all of the symptoms of sadness whether or not it is accompanied by a cause. Consequently, many more people are being diagnosed with clinical depression.

The ascendancy of depressive disorder is a major social trend manifested in a variety of ways:

Amount of depression in the community. Many of researchers claim that substantial and growing proportions of the population suffer from depressive disorder. Estimates from epidemiological studies indicate that major depression afflicts about 10% of adults in the United States each year and nearly a fifth of the population at some point in their lives. Rates among women are even higher, about twice as high as in men. Depending on the definition employed, depression can afflict as many as half of the members of some groups, such as female adolescents and the elderly. Moreover, these numbers seem to be steadily growing. For the past several decades, each successive birth cohort has reported more depressive disorders than previous generations showed. Although these rising rates are more likely to be an artifact of the way community surveys measure this condition than to reflect an actual increase, there is a widespread perception that depressive disorder is growing at an alarming pace.

The Ubiquity of Depression

Number of patients in treatment for depression. The number of persons treated for depression in the United States has grown explosively in recent years. Most depressed people are treated in outpatient settings, where treatment of depression increased by 300% between 1987 and 1997. By 1997, fully 40% of all psychotherapy patients, double the percentage of a decade before, had diagnoses of a mood disorder, the larger category that comprises mainly depression. The overall percentage of the population in treatment for depression in a particular year grew from 2.1% in the early 1980s to 3.7% in the early 2000s, an increase of 76% in just 20 years. Some groups experienced a much greater increase; for example, in just the period between

1992 and 1998, health care providers diagnosed 107% more elderly persons with depression.

Prescription of antidepressant medication. Although medication has been a common treatment for life problems since the 1950s, its use has undergone a staggering growth in recent years. Antidepressant medications, such as Prozac, Paxil, Zoloft, and Effexor, are now among the largest selling prescription drugs of any sort. Their use among adults nearly tripled between 1988 and 2000. In any given month, 10% of women and 4% of men now use these drugs. During the 1990s, spending for antidepressants increased by 600% in the United States, exceeding $7 billion annually by the year 2000.

Estimates of the social cost of depression. Depression is believed to be the source of huge social costs. The World Health Organization (WHO), the leading international body that deals with health, projects that by 2020 depression will become the

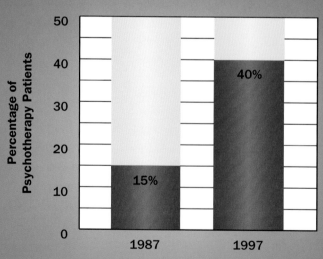

Outpatient Treatment of Depression

Psychotherapy Patients with Diagnosis of Mood Disorder

Taken from: Allan Horwitz, *Loss of Sadness*, Oxford University Press, 2007.

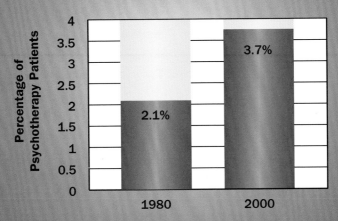

People in Treatment for Depression

Percentage of Psychotherapy Patients

1980: 2.1%
2000: 3.7%

Taken from: Allan Horwitz, *Loss of Sadness*, Oxford University Press, 2007.

second leading cause of worldwide disability, behind only heart disease. The WHO estimates that depression is already the leading cause of disability for 15- to 44-year-olds. In the United States, economists estimate that depression is responsible for $43 billion in costs every year.

Scientific publications on depression. Research on depression has become a major industry. In 1966, 703 articles containing the word depression in their titles were published in medical journals. In 1980, the year in which the American Psychiatric Association (APA) published its landmark third edition of the *Diagnostic and Statistical Manual of Mental Disorders (DSM-III)* with new definitions of depressive disorder, 2,754 articles on depression were published. This number steadily increased over the following 15 years, and then exploded in the mid-1990s. By 2005, there were 8,677 articles about depression published, more than 12 times the number in 1966. The number of articles concerned with depression is now far higher than any other psychiatric diagnosis and has grown far more rapidly than the general growth in psychiatric research publications.

Media attention to depression. Depression has become a central concern in the culture more generally. Popular television shows, best-selling books, and major articles in national magazines often feature this illness. Many memoirs about personal experiences of depression, including William Styron's *Darkness Visible*, Kay Jamison's *An Unquiet Mind*, Elizabeth Wurtzel's *Prozac Nation*, and Andrew Solomon's *The Noonday Demon*, have reached the best-seller list. A look at the new books in the psychology sections of bookstores reveals a virtual tidal wave of books on how to prevent or cope with depression of all sorts. The acclaimed television series, *The Sopranos*, features as its central character a Mafia boss who has—among other psychiatric conditions—depression and whose consumption of antidepressant medications is a major theme of the show. A number of prominent public personalities, including Tipper Gore, Mike Wallace, and Brooke Shields, have received massive publicity after disclosing their depressive conditions.

Normal Versus Disordered Sadness

Although the belief that depression is a widespread phenomenon is new, the symptoms we now associate with it, including intense sadness and the many other emotional experiences and physical symptoms that often accompany sadness, have been noted since the beginning of recorded medical history. Yet, in attempting to understand the recent upsurge in diagnosed depressive disorder, it is important to recognize that until recently, two broad types of conditions that manifest these same symptoms were sharply distinguished from each other. One, normal sadness, or sadness "with cause," was associated with experiences of loss or other painful circumstances that seemed to be the obvious causes of distress. The response to such normal reactions was to offer support, to help the individual cope and move on despite the loss, and to avoid confusing the person's sadness with illness.

The other kind of condition, traditionally known as *melancholia*, or depression "without cause," was a medical disorder distinguished from normal sadness by the fact that the patient's symptoms occurred despite there being no appropriate reason for them in the patient's circumstances. These conditions were relatively rare but tended to be long lasting and recurrent. Because they were not proportional reactions to actual events, such conditions were assumed to stem from some sort of internal defect or dysfunction that required professional attention. Yet these pathological conditions involve the same sorts of symptoms—such as sadness, insomnia, social withdrawal, loss of appetite, lack of interest in usual activities, and so on—associated with intense normal sadness.

Medications for depression include Prozac. Use of antidepressants in the United States costs $43 billion annually.

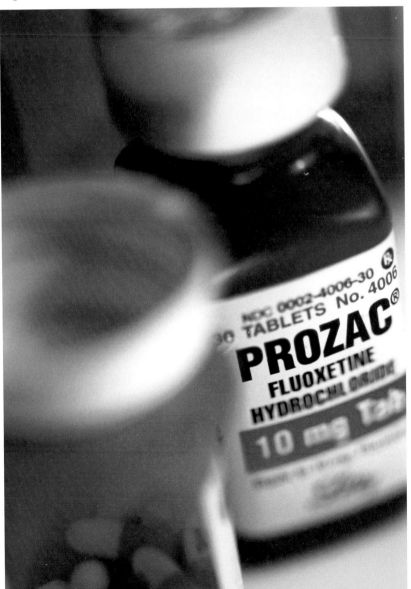

This separation of normal sadness and depressive disorder is a sensible and legitimate, indeed a crucial, one. It is consistent not only with the general distinction between normality and disorder used in medicine and traditional psychiatry but also with common sense, and it has both clinical and scientific importance. Yet contemporary psychiatry has come to largely ignore this distinction.

We argue that the recent explosion of putative depressive disorder, in fact, does not stem primarily from a real rise in this condition. Instead, it is largely a product of conflating the two conceptually distinct categories of normal sadness and depressive disorder and thus classifying many instances of normal sadness as mental disorders. The current "epidemic," although the result of many social factors, has been made possible by a changed psychiatric definition of depressive disorder that often allows the classification of sadness as disease, even when it is not. . . .

Faulty Definition of Depressive Disorder

There are no obvious circumstances that would explain a recent upsurge in depressive disorder. The most commonly heard suggestions—such as that modern life is less socially anchored and involves more alienation or that media constantly expose us to extremes of wealth and beauty that cause us to feel inadequate by comparison—would tend to explain only normal sadness reactions . . . , not the massive growth of a mental disorder. No environmental pathogen that might have resulted in a real increase in physiologically, psychologically, or socially induced brain malfunctions has been identified or even theorized. Certainly, progress in effectively treating depressive disorder with psychotropic medication has resulted in increased treatment of a condition about which physicians believe they can at least do some good, and perhaps it has motivated diagnosis of formerly ambiguous cases as depression in the hope of offering effective treatment. But that does not by itself explain the vast growth in the numbers of people who seemingly have and are treated for this disorder; better treatments do not usually lead to a substantial increase in disease prevalence. Nor would improved treatments explain the results of epidemiological studies that bypass patients and directly interview community members not in treatment. Thus the seeming explosion of cases of depressive disorder is puzzling. What has happened to create the appearance of this epidemic?

What has happened, we argue, is largely diagnostic inflation based on a relatively new definition of depressive disorder that is flawed and that, combined with other developments in society, has dramatically expanded the domain of presumed disorder. . . .

Symptom-Based Definition

But how can something as simple and limited as a definition have substantial consequences for such a field as psychiatry and thus for the media that popularize its claims and findings and for the thinking of society at large that relies on its expertise? In response to criticisms during the 1960s and 1970s that different psychiatrists would not diagnose the same person with the same symptoms in the same way (this problem was known as the "unreliability" of diagnosis), in 1980 the DSM began to use lists of symptoms to establish clear definitions for each disorder.

Almost all mental health professionals across a variety of settings, from hospital clinics to private practices, now use these formal definitions for clinical diagnosis. Moreover, these definitions have percolated out of the mental health clinical arena and are used in epidemiological studies of disorder in the community, in research studies of treatment outcomes, in marketing of antidepressant medications, in preventive efforts in schools, in screening in general medical practice, in court proceedings, and in many other settings. In effect, these DSM definitions have become the authoritative arbiter of what is and is not considered mental disorder throughout our society. What might seem like abstract, distant, technical issues concerning these definitions in fact have important consequences for individuals and how their suffering is understood and addressed.

The fact that these symptom-based definitions are the foundation of the entire mental health research and treatment enterprise makes their validity critically important. Psychiatric research and treatment are like an upside-down pyramid, and the *DSM* definitions of mental disorders that determine who is counted as disordered are the one small point on which the soundness of the entire pyramid rests. Even the best clinical history taking and diagnostic interviewing or the best research sample selection, experimental design, and statistical analysis of data will not produce meaningful results if they use an invalid definition of disorder that mixes normal and abnormal features.

[Greek mathematician] Archimedes famously boasted, "Give me a lever long enough, and a pivot on which to rest it, and I will move the earth." In modern psychiatry, definitions move the treatment and research firmament, and modern clinicians with an invalidly broad definition can move [a] diagnosed disorder to virtually whatever level they desire, especially when they deal with a disorder such as depression that features such symptoms as sadness, insomnia, and fatigue, which are widespread among nondisordered people. Thus the recent focus in psychiatry on reliability of diagnosis based on symptoms has been pursued at some cost to validity—that is, whether the diagnosis represents a correct attribution of disorder. The *DSM*'s criteria for Major Depressive Disorder are one instance in which increased reliability has had the inadvertent side effect of creating substantial new validity problems.

SEVEN

Bipolar Disorder Is Underdiagnosed in Youth

Demitri F. Papolos

> Demitri F. Papolos is director of research of the Juvenile Bipolar Research Foundation and an associate professor of psychiatry at the Albert Einstein College of Medicine in New York City. He also wrote *The Bipolar Child* and *Overcoming Depression*. In the following viewpoint Papolos reports that rates of childhood-onset bipolar disorder have been rising since 1940. Children with bipolar disorder exhibit ultra-ultra rapid, or ultradian, swings of mood and energy several times a day and have prolonged temper tantrums and are sometimes violent. Children as young as six and ten are exhibiting these symptoms. However, these important symptoms are not listed as prominent characteristics of bipolar disorder in children in the *DSM-IV*, the diagnostic manual by which doctors and psychiatrists critique and track mental illnesses. As the *DSM-IV* has not been revised since 2000, Papolos recommends it be updated in order to recognize differences in diagnosing bipolar disorder in children versus adults.

Over the last decade, mood disorders in children and adolescents have received increased recognition. However, in contrast to the growing body of literature on non-bipolar depression,

Demitri F. Papolos, "Childhood-Onset Bipolar Disorder: Under-diagnosed, Under-treated and Under Discussion," *NARSAD Research Newsletter*, vol. 17, Fall 2005. Reproduced by permission.

Number of Cases of Bipolar Disorder in Children and Adolescents

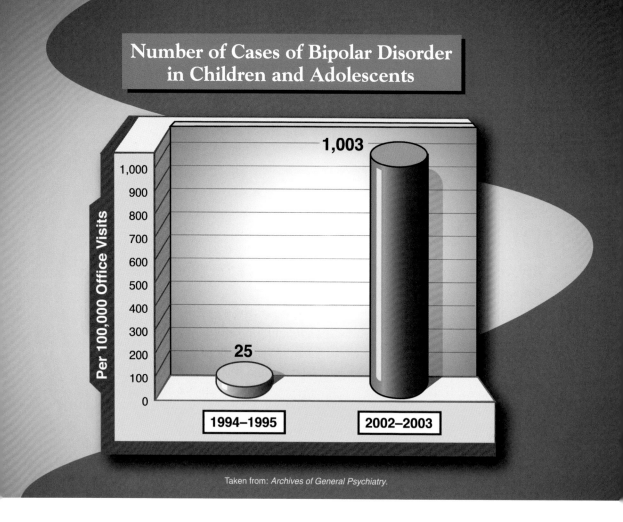

Taken from: *Archives of General Psychiatry.*

bipolar disorder [BPD] (manic-depression) has been relatively neglected, and its diagnosis in childhood remains the subject of great controversy in the fields of clinical child psychiatry and psychology.

A host of problems has contributed to this unfortunate state of affairs—not the least of which is the misconception that bipolar disorders in the pediatric age group are rare and unlikely to be seen before puberty. From at least the 1930s onward, standard clinical textbooks have omitted reference to the condition. This prevailing view has persisted to the present day, despite clinical observations of mania and melancholia in the young since ancient times. Compelling reports from general population and family studies show progressively higher rates of early onset mood disorders in successive generations since 1940.

The fact that *DSM-IV*—the diagnostic manual whose criteria are used by mental health practitioners across the country to make psychiatric diagnoses—defines bipolar disorder no differently in children than it does in adults, further compounds this outlook.

The last revision of the *DSM* took place over six years ago [in 2000], whereas most of what we now know about childhood-onset bipolar disorder (COBPD) did not reach the literature until after the completion of the most recent revision.

Differences Between Childhood- and Adult-Onset Forms of Bipolar Disorder

While adult-onset and juvenile-onset forms of bipolar disorder have certain similar features in common, the stark difference in the frequency and duration of mood/energy cycles, known as ultra-ultra rapid or ultradian cycles, between the adult and childhood-onset forms has had a confounding affect on clinical diagnostic practice. The juvenile form of the disorder is also wrought by prolonged temper tantrums and rages, as well as the frequent overlap of symptoms of other commonly diagnosed childhood disorders.

Diagnostic and treatment studies of children with bipolar disorder have all observed the tendency towards ultra-ultra rapid or ultradian cycles—rapid swings of mood and energy multiple times within the day—one of the key hallmarks of COBPD. Over 75% of individuals with COBPD have rapid, continuous, or ultra-ultra rapid (ultradian) cycles of mood. Clinically, this phenomenon can be observed as rapid and dramatic shifts in mood and energy that often cause parents to describe their children as unpredictable, alternating between belligerent, nasty, hostile, and silly, goofy, giddy mood states. This Dr. Jekyll and Mr. Hyde portrait of behavior distinguishes COBPD from other disruptive disorders of childhood with which it is commonly confused.

Labile, unstable, and rapidly changeable mood is particularly striking among young patients under 10 years of age. In one of the largest studies of childhood-onset bipolar disorder, the frequent occurrence of ultra-ultra rapid or ultradian cycling in mood and energy was reported by parents as being present as early as age six in a sizable percent of the sample.

Need to Revise *DSM-IV* Criteria
Although this is a key feature of the condition for a majority, it is not included in the current diagnostic criteria of the *DSM-IV*,

Temper tantrums are a prominent feature of childhood-onset bipolar disorder (COBPD).

making it likely that not more than one quarter of children with early-onset bipolar disorder will be properly diagnosed.

The addition of ultradian or ultra-ultra rapid-cycling to these criteria would certainly serve to improve current diagnostic practices and lead to a greater appreciation of the rate of pediatric bipolar disorder in the general population. A manic episode may be unrecognized if rapid shifts of mood and energy and labile presentation are not viewed as salient characteristics of the disorder. It is therefore clear that there exists an urgent public health need to revise the *DSM-IV* criteria for COBPD.

Temper Tantrums and Rages

Severe, prolonged temper tantrums with aggressive, often violent and destructive rages have diagnostic value, noting that the energy manifested by tantrums of bipolar youths can be extraordinary to witness, hard to believe, and difficult to imitate.

Such rages have been found to be one of the prominent clinical features of COBPD in a large sample of juvenile-onset cases. A full 92% of the sample had recurrent rageful and often violent tantrums lasting longer than 45 minutes with oppositional/defiant behaviors. Bossy, demanding, intense, explosive, aggressive, and intimidating were some of the most common terms used by parents to describe the behavior and demeanor of their children.

In contrast to existing diagnostic criteria of the *DSM-IV*, that require persistence of symptoms, a more fitting prototype of bipolar disorder in childhood would incorporate its unstable and ultra-ultra rapid-cycling clinical presentation, as well as the tendency towards temper tantrums and prolonged rages.

The Comorbidity of COBPD with Attention Deficit Disorder and Oppositional Defiant Disorder

In addition to differences in phenomenology [observable manifestations], course, and cycling pattern, symptomatic overlap with other conditions, including attention deficit disorder with hyperactivity (ADHD) and oppositional defiant disorder, is apparently a cardinal feature of COBPD.

Comorbidity of Mental Illness in Children

Study: of 43 manic children	**Results:** 94 percent also had ADHD
Study: of 120 bipolar children	**Results:** 93 percent also had ADHD 90 percent had oppositional defiant disorder as well

Taken from: Demitri F. Papolos, "Childhood-Onset Bipolar Disorder: Under-Diagnosed, Under-Treated, and Under Discussion," National Alliance for Research on Schizophrenia and Depression, Fall 2005.

Distinguishing children with COBPD from those with ADHD by clinical assessment alone is difficult since three of the seven criteria for COBPD are shared with ADHD. These criteria are: distractibility, physical agitation, and talkativeness.

In a 1995 study of 43 manic children, aged 12 or younger, who were referred to an outpatient psychopharmacology clinic, 94% of the sample also met full *DSM-III-R* criteria for ADHD.

In a study of parent reports, which retrospectively examined the evolution of symptomatology in a group of 120 children and adolescents (ages 3–18) diagnosed with bipolar disorder, 93% were reported to have *DSM-IV* ADHD, and over 90% met full criteria for oppositional defiant disorder.

Family-genetic studies are uniquely suited for the evaluation of such complicated diagnostic pictures. A separate study found that both disorders were elevated in relatives of pro-bands diagnosed with ADHD and BPD and, a significant percentage of the relatives had both conditions. A phenomenon, known as "co-segregation," whereby the conditions segregate together in families, suggests that COBPD and ADHD may be transmitted together, not independently, at least in a subgroup of families.

What is beginning to emerge is a view that this same phenomenon can be observed between COBPD and a number of childhood psychiatric disorders including conduct disorders,

Tourette's syndrome, obsessive-compulsive disorder, and other anxiety disorders.

Epidemiological and Naturalistic Follow-Up Studies

Historical biases stifled any attempt to quantify COBPD rates in juvenile epidemiological samples, and until recently, almost all available data on bipolar disorder in childhood and adolescence had been derived from small samples of patients and anecdotal reports.

The first large-scale review of the world literature that took issue with prevailing diagnostic practices was a meta-analysis of 2,168 cases in 1994. It concluded that while clinical features of pediatric and adult bipolar disorder have similarities, pediatric cases cannot be defined solely by features characteristic of the adult disorder. This review and subsequent diagnostic studies have paved the way for a re-evaluation of the long-standing myths that have largely obscured our understanding of the condition and its rate in the general population.

The first report in the literature, on a community sample of adolescents, was published in 1988. These youth had rates of hypomania as high as 13%, endorsed four or more manic symptoms of at least 2 days duration and, compared to the rest of the sample, had significantly higher rates of attention deficit, conduct, and anxiety disorders, as well as psychotic symptoms.

In 1995, the first major epidemiological study of bipolar disorder was conducted in a sample of over 1700 Oregon high school students. Researchers found a lifetime prevalence of bipolar disorders of 0.90–1.41%—a rate equivalent to that seen in the adult population. When less stringent episode duration criteria were applied to this group, the rates rose to 9.0%, comparable to earlier reports, and to recent findings in a study of an adult population with hypomania.

More than half of the bipolar subjects in the Oregon study had received some form of mental health treatment, yet only one subject had been treated with lithium, suggesting that many of these students were not recognized as having bipolar disorder by mental health professionals with whom they came into contact.

Need for Better Diagnosis in Children

Within the complete and incorrect criteria being used to diagnose bipolar disorder in youth by the majority of mental health practitioners around the country, coupled with the burgeoning administration of stimulants and antidepressants to the general pediatric population and their potential for serious adverse effects, a public health nightmare is brewing.

When we take the high frequency of overlapping symptoms of two commonly accepted and diagnosed conditions in child psychiatry, together with the one week duration requirement of mood episodes used to make the diagnosis by *DSM-IV* criteria, combined with the historical bias against diagnosing BPD before puberty, we need not search further for reasons as to why this condition is so poorly recognized and so often misdiagnosed in childhood.

Since revisions of *DSM-IV* are not planned until [2012], it behooves pediatricians, pediatric neurologists and child psychiatrists alike to become more aware of this area of diagnostic confusion and controversy. The stakes are clearly quite high.

EIGHT

Antidepressant Use Must Be Monitored to Be Effective

Richard A. Friedman

Richard A. Friedman is a professor of psychiatry at Weill Cornell Medical College in New York. In the following article Friedman explains that risk from long-term use of antidepressants is low. Although suicidal thoughts and nonlethal suicide attempts in adolescents who use antidepressants have increased, the lifetime risk of actual suicide in depressed adults is far lower than the risk of suicide by adults receiving no treatment for their illness. So far no evidence has proved that long-term use of antidepressants carries a risk, but physicians and the public need reliable research on long-term use of antidepressants, especially when use initiates during adolescence and throughout adulthood. To keep drug testing results accurate and ethical, Friedman encourages skepticism of drug research paid for by pharmaceutical companies.

"I've grown up on medication," my patient Julie told me recently. "I don't have a sense of who I really am without it."

At 31, she had been on one antidepressant or another nearly continuously since she was 14. There was little question that she had very serious depression and had survived several suicide attempts. In fact, she credited the medication with saving her life.

Richard A. Friedman, "Who Are We? Coming of Age on Antidepressants," *New York Times*, April 15, 2008, p. F5 (L). Copyright © 2008 by The New York Times Company. Reprinted with permission.

But now she was raising an equally fundamental question: how the drugs might have affected her psychological development and core identity. It was not an issue I had seriously considered before. Most of my patients, who are adults, developed their psychiatric problems after they had a pretty clear idea of who they were as individuals. During treatment, most of them could tell me whether they were back to their normal baseline.

Julie could certainly remember what depression felt like, but she could not recall feeling well except during her long treatment with antidepressant medications. And since she had not grown up before getting depressed, she could not gauge the hypothetical effects of antidepressants on her emotional and psychological development.

Risk of Antidepressant Treatment Is Low

Her experience is far from unique. Since their emergence in the late 1980s, serotonin reuptake inhibitors like Prozac and Zoloft have become some of the most widely prescribed drugs in the world, for depressed teenagers as well as adults. Because depression is often a chronic, recurring illness, there are certain to be many young people, like Julie, who are coming of age on these newer antidepressants.

We know a lot about the course of untreated depression, probably more than we do about very long-term antidepressant use in this population. We know, for example, that depression in young people is a very serious problem; suicide is the third-leading cause of death in adolescents, not to mention the untold suffering and impaired functioning this disease exacts.

By contrast, the risk of antidepressant treatment is small. A 2004 review by the Food and Drug Administration [FDA], analyzing clinical trials of the drugs, did show an elevated risk of suicidal thinking and nonlethal suicide attempts in young people taking antidepressants—3.5 percent, compared with 1.7 percent of those taking a placebo. But since the lifetime risk of actual suicide in depressed people ranges from 2.2 to 12 percent, risk from treatment is dwarfed by the risks of the disease itself.

Still, what do we know about the effects of, say, 15 to 20 years of antidepressant drug treatment that begins in adolescence or childhood? Not enough.

Long-Term Drug Testing

The reason has to do with the way drugs are tested and approved. To get F.D.A. approval, a drug has to beat a placebo in two

Depression is a serious problem among young people, with suicide being the third leading cause of death among adolescents.

randomized clinical trials that typically involve a few hundred subjects who are treated for relatively short periods, usually 4 to 12 weeks.

So drugs are approved based on short-term studies for what turns out to be long-term—often lifelong—use in the world of clinical practice. The longest maintenance study to date of one of the newer antidepressants, Effexor, lasted only two years and showed the drug to be superior to a placebo in preventing relapses of depression.

What do I say to a depressed patient who is doing well after five years on such a drug but can't stop without a depressive relapse and who wants reassurance that the drug has no long-term adverse effects? I usually say that we have no evidence that the drug poses a risk with long-term use; and since the risk of un-

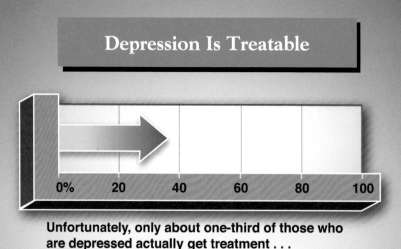

Depression Is Treatable

Unfortunately, only about one-third of those who are depressed actually get treatment . . .

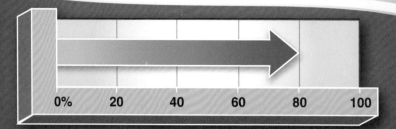

while up to 80–90 percent who do get treatment can feel better, usually within a few weeks.

Taken from: www.allaboutdepression.com.

treated depression is much greater than the hypothetical risk of the drug, it makes sense to stay on it.

This large gap in our clinical knowledge is compounded by the public's growing and well-founded skepticism about research sponsored by drug makers. A study in the January 2008 issue of *The New England Journal of Medicine*, involving 74 clinical trials with 12 antidepressants, found that 97 percent of positive studies were published, versus 12 percent of negative studies.

Clearly, physicians and the public need much better data on the safety and efficacy of drugs after they hit the market, which at present consists mainly of anecdotes and case reports.

Congress recently reauthorized the Prescription Drug User Fee Act, which will expand the F.D.A.'s post-marketing drug surveillance, though I think it did not go far enough in mandating the use of powerful epidemiological strategies to monitor drugs over the long term.

Beyond these concerns, there are other important issues to consider in long-term use of antidepressants, especially in young people. One patient, a woman in her mid-20s, told me that she felt pressured by her boyfriend to have sex more often than she wanted. "I've always had a low sex drive," she said.

For the past eight years she had been taking Zoloft, which like all the antidepressants in its class is known to lower libido and to interfere with sexual performance. She had understandably mistaken the side effect of the drug for her "normal" sexual desire and was shocked when I explained it: "And I thought it was just me!"

This just underscores how tricky it can be to use psychotropic drugs during adolescence—when the brain is still developing, when one's identity is still a work in progress.

The drugs save lives, and we often have no choice but to use them—even if we have questions about their long-term use. But the questions are big ones, and we owe it to our patients to try to answer them.

NINE

Positive Psychology May Help Treat Mental Illness

Harvard Medical School

The following article from Harvard Medical School describes positive psychology, a form of psychotherapy that highlights the positive aspects of a person's life. In positive psychology treatment, a person identifies personal strengths and positive aspects of their lives. People are encouraged to keep a journal of positive achievements, list three good things that happen to them each day, write a letter to someone they are grateful to, focus on what they did today rather than what they did not do or need to do, and use positive language in daily activities. Research on the success of positive psychology is limited; however preliminary results are encouraging.

Positive psychology is sometimes dismissed as so much happy talk. But practitioners say that their techniques provide a much-needed balance to psychiatry's traditional focus on psychic pain and pathology.

The term "positive psychology" is a broad one, encompassing a variety of techniques that encourage people to identify and further develop their own positive emotions, experiences, and character traits. In many ways, positive psychology builds on key tenets of humanistic psychology. [Psychologist] Carl Rog-

"Positive Psychology in Practice," *Harvard Mental Health Letter*, vol. 24, May 2008, pp. 1–3. © 2008 Harvard University. Reproduced by permission.

ers' client-centered therapy, for example, was based on the theory that people could improve their lives by expressing their authentic selves. And [psychologist] Abraham Maslow identified traits of self-actualized people that are similar to the character strengths identified and used in some positive psychology interventions.

Complement Traditional Therapy

Although initially developed as a way to advance well-being and optimal functioning in healthy people, positive psychology techniques are now being promoted as a complement to more traditional forms of therapy. For example, University of Pennsylvania psychologist Martin E.P. Seligman, a well-known advocate of positive psychology, has described its core philosophy as a "build what's strong" approach that can augment the "fix what's wrong" approach of more traditional psychotherapy.

Another pioneer in the field, Harvard psychiatrist George E. Vaillant, sees positive psychology as a way to encourage patients to focus on positive emotions and build strengths, supplementing psychotherapy that focuses on negative emotions, like anger and sorrow. In a recent talk about positive psychology, Dr. Vaillant cited the example of a standard psychiatric textbook used by psychiatrists and clinical psychologists. The textbook, he says, contains roughly a million lines of text, with thousands of lines devoted to anxiety and depression, and hundreds discussing terror, shame, guilt, anger, and fear. But only five lines in the textbook discuss hope, only one mentions joy, and not a single line mentions compassion or love.

To counter the traditional focus on pathology, Seligman and another psychologist, Christopher Peterson, have formalized the tenets of positive psychology in a book, *Character Strengths and Virtues: A Handbook and Classification (CSV)*, which they created as a counterpoint to the *Diagnostic and Statistical Manual of Mental Disorders, Fourth Edition (DSM-IV)*. Just as the *DSM-IV* classifies a range of psychiatric disorders, the *CSV* provides details and classifications for various strengths that enable people to thrive. The book identifies 24 character strengths, like curiosity and zest, organized according to six overarching virtues, such as wisdom and courage.

Positive Counseling Strategies

A number of different counseling and coaching strategies rely on aspects of positive psychology. Although its impossible to review all of them in a single article, a few examples can help to provide a taste of how they may complement more traditional therapies.

Well-Being Therapy

As its name implies, well-being therapy tries to promote recovery from depression and other affective disorders by having a patient focus on and promote the positive, as well as alleviating negative aspects of life. Developed by Giovanni Fava at the University of Bologna in Italy, well-being therapy is based in large part on the work of psychologist Carol Ryff and her multidimensional model of subjective well-being. Ryff's model consists of six tenets: mastery of the environment, personal growth, purpose in life, autonomy, self-acceptance, and positive relationships.

In practical terms, well-being therapy is much like cognitive behavioral therapy. A patient keeps a journal to keep track of and recognize the positive events that occur each day. Next the patient starts recognizing negative thoughts and beliefs that distract from or disrupt positive events. The ultimate goal is to challenge and eventually change negative ways of thinking, to enable positive events to have more of an impact on the patient's life.

Positive Psychotherapy

Seligman and colleagues at the University of Pennsylvania developed positive psychotherapy as a way to treat depression by building positive emotions, character strengths, and sense of meaning, not just by reducing negative symptoms such as sadness. This therapy uses a combination of 12 exercises (such as the following) that can be practiced individually or in groups.

Using your signature strengths. Identify your top five strengths . . . and try to use them in some new way daily.

Three good things. Every evening, write down three good things that happened that day and think about why they happened.

Gratitude visit. Write a letter to someone explaining why you feel grateful for something they've done or said. Read the letter to the recipient, either in person or over the phone.

This is one of the few forms of positive psychotherapy that has been tested in a randomized controlled trial. The study found that some exercises are more beneficial than others (see [below] "Does positive psychology work?" for details).

Proponents of positive psychology techniques maintain that focusing on building positive emotions is an effective complement to traditional therapy, which tends to deal with negative emotions such as anger and psychic pain.

Integrating Positive Psychology in Practice

Psychologist Carol Kauffman, director of the Coaching and Positive Psychology Initiative at Harvard's McLean Hospital, recently discussed four techniques for integrating the principles of positive psychology into more traditional types of individual or group therapy.

Reverse the focus from negative to positive. Most people tend to dwell on negative events or emotions and ignore the positive ones—and therapy can encourage this. One way to reverse the focus is to use techniques aimed at shifting attention to more positive aspects of life. For example, take a mental spotlight each night and scan over the events of the day, thinking about what went right. Another tip is to compile "I did it" lists instead of only writing down what needs to be done.

Develop a language of strength. Therapists and patients often talk about pain, conflict, and anger. Although these are all aspects of life, it may be harder for people to talk about or even identify more positive qualities and personal strengths.

Kauffman and other positive psychology practitioners often use strength coaching while advising patients. Just as an athlete exercises certain muscles to become stronger, the theory is that people who use their strengths regularly will function better in life. To boost mental facility, Kauffman recommends that people identify one top strength and then use it at least once a day.

Balance the positive and negative. It's also important for people to identify and foster the positive for themselves and others in order to provide a balance to the negative. For example, business executives may mix praise with criticism when evaluating employees to nurture their growth.

Build strategies that foster hope. Finding ways to foster hope in someone may increase that person's ability to deal with adversity and overcome a challenge. One way to cultivate hope is to reduce the scope of the problem—perhaps by breaking it down into components that can be tackled one at a time. Another way is to identify skills and coping mechanisms that would enable someone to overcome a particular challenge, and then provide a way to build them.

Does Positive Psychology Work?

Proponents of positive psychology tend to cite studies showing that optimistic or happy people are healthier, more successful, and live longer than other people. Critics counter that people may have inborn temperaments that function a bit like set-points, and that interventions aimed at making them happier will only work for a limited time. Eventually, the critics claim, people return to their baseline level of happiness.

A 2005 review of the studies published about positive psychology interventions found that only one involved people with clinical depression—and that study was small, and the intervention was not tested against a control. The study enrolled 16 people who met the criteria for clinical depression according to their scores on the Beck Depression Inventory and the Hamilton Rating Scale of Depression. Participants met weekly for 15 weeks to discuss readings about topics such as how to increase satisfaction with health and improve self-esteem. All 13 people who completed the study were reassessed at the end of the intervention; none of them met the criteria for clinical depression.

Since then, only one large randomized controlled trial of a positive psychology intervention for people with clinical depression has been published. After two preliminary studies found positive psychotherapy (PPT) to be promising, Seligman and colleagues conducted a randomized controlled trial involving 411 participants that compared five different PPT exercises with a control exercise, all of which were administered over the Internet and could be completed in one week. Participants were assessed before the intervention and then periodically afterward for six months.

At the six-month mark, participants were rated by the Steen Happiness Index and the Center for Epidemiologic Studies Depression Scale. Those completing the "using your signature strengths" and "three good things" exercises rated significantly happier and less depressed than the control group. The "gratitude visit" exercise also created positive changes, but only for one month. The two other exercises and the control exercise created briefer and transient effects.

Research Is Limited

Most other studies have been short-term in nature (several lasted six to 10 weeks, and one lasted three days) and have involved people who did not have psychiatric diagnoses. This means it remains unclear whether positive psychology techniques will help people suffering from depression and other psychiatric disorders.

Another limitation in the research so far is that investigators have evaluated mostly individual strategies, but positive psychology interventions usually combine several techniques at once. It's also unclear how best to combine positive psychology interventions with more traditional types of therapy, such as cognitive behavioral therapy, or with medication.

Although the jury is still out on the clinical impact of positive psychology, leaders in the field are encouraging patients and clinicians to give positive techniques a try. After all, there are few risks involved when someone discovers his or her strengths or focuses on the positive side of life—and there may be valuable benefits.

TEN

Legislation Is Needed to Protect the Mentally Ill

World Health Organization

> The World Health Organization (WHO) sets standards for health care, shapes agendas, advises nations on health issues, and monitors health trends. In the following document, WHO advises countries to adopt mental health legislation to protect the human rights of people with mental illness. People who suffer from mental illness are vulnerable to ridicule and social stigma. According to WHO, 25 percent of countries have no national mental health legislation. WHO argues that effective and enforced legislation allows the mentally ill access to suitable educational, employment, and housing opportunities.

Mental health legislation is necessary for protecting the rights of people with mental disorders, who are a vulnerable section of society. They face stigma, discrimination and marginalization in all societies, and this increases the likelihood that their human rights will be violated. Mental disorders can sometimes affect people's decision-making capacities and they may not always seek or accept treatment for their problems. Rarely, people with mental disorders may pose a risk to themselves and others because of impaired decision-making abilities. The risk of violence or harm associated with mental disorders is relatively small.

Mental Health Legislation and Human Rights, Geneva, Switzerland: World Health Organization, 2003.
Copyright © World Health Organization 2003. All rights reserved. Reproduced by permission.

Common misconceptions on this matter should not be allowed to influence mental health legislation.

Mental health legislation can provide a legal framework for addressing critical issues such as the community integration of persons with mental disorders, the provision of care of high quality, the improvement of access to care, the protection of civil rights and the protection and promotion of rights in other critical areas such as housing, education and employment. Legislation can also play an important role in promoting mental health and preventing mental disorders. Mental health legislation is thus more than care and treatment legislation that is narrowly limited to the provision of treatment in institution-based health services.

There is no national mental health legislation in 25% of countries with nearly 31% of the world's population, although countries with a federal system of governance may have state mental health laws. Of the countries in which there is mental health legislation, half have national laws that were passed after 1990. Some 15% have legislation that was enacted before 1960, i.e. before most of the currently used treatment modalities became available (World Health Organization, 2001). The existence of mental health legislation does not necessarily guarantee the protection of the human rights of people with mental disorders. In

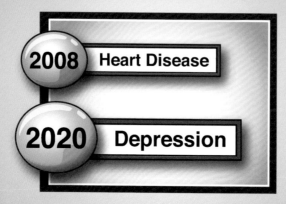

Leading Cause of Death Worldwide

2008 Heart Disease

2020 Depression

Taken from: World Health Organization projection.

some countries, indeed, mental health legislation contains provisions that lead to the violation of human rights.

Legislation Provides Public Awareness

Legislation for protecting the rights of people with mental disorders may be either consolidated or dispersed. Most countries have consolidated mental health legislation, in which all the relevant issues are incorporated in a single legislative document. This has the advantage of ease of adoption and enactment. Moreover, the process of drafting, adopting and implementing such legislation provides a good opportunity for raising public awareness and educating policy-makers and society in general.

The alternative is to insert provisions related to mental disorders into other legislation. For example, legislative provisions for protecting the employment rights of persons with mental disorders could be inserted in relevant employment legislation. This approach can increase the possibility of implementing provisions for the benefit of persons with mental disorders because the provisions are part of legislation that benefits a much wider range of people. However, such dispersed legislation is difficult to enact as it requires amendments and changes to multiple legislative documents. Moreover, the potential exists for important issues to be omitted.

A combined approach is most likely to address the complexity of the needs of people with mental disorders, i.e. specific mental health legislation can be complemented by more general legislation in which mental health issues are addressed.

Mental Health Regulations

Mental health legislation should be viewed as a process rather than as an event that occurs just once in many decades. This allows it to be amended in response to advances in the treatment of mental disorders and to developments in service delivery systems. However, frequent amendments to legislation are not feasible because of the time and financial resources required and the need to consult all stakeholders.

A possible solution is to lay down regulations that are separate from legislation but can be enforced through it. Legislation can include provision for the establishment of regulations and can outline the procedure for modifying them. The most important advantage of regulations is that they do not require lawmakers to be repeatedly voting for amendments. In some countries, executive decrees and service orders are used as an alternative to regulations.

Mental health legislation is essential for complementing and reinforcing mental health policy and providing a legal framework for meeting its goals. Such legislation can protect human rights, enhance the quality of mental health services and promote the integration of persons with mental disorders into communities. These goals are an integral part of national mental health policies. . . .

The key components of mental health legislation are discussed below. They are neither exclusive nor exhaustive but represent the most important issues that should be adequately addressed in legislation.

Provisions in Mental Health Legislation

The principle of the least restrictive alternative requires that persons are always offered treatment in settings that have the least possible effect on their personal freedom and their status and privileges in the community, including their ability to continue to work, move about and conduct their affairs. In practice, this means promoting community-based treatments and using institutional treatment settings only in rare circumstances. If institutional treatment is necessary, the legislation should encourage voluntary admission and treatment and allow involuntary admission and treatment only in exceptional circumstances. The development of community-based treatment facilities is a prerequisite for putting this principle into practice.

The legislation should guarantee to persons with mental disorders that confidentiality exists in respect of all information obtained in a clinical context. The laws should explicitly prevent disclosure, examination or transmission of patients' mental health records without their consent.

The principle of free and informed consent to treatment should be enshrined in the legislation. Treatment without consent (involuntary treatment) should be permitted only under exceptional circumstances (which must be outlined). The legislation should incorporate adequate procedural mechanisms that protect the rights of persons with mental disorders who are being treated involuntarily, and should permit clinical and research trials only if patients have given free and informed consent. This applies equally to patients admitted involuntarily to mental health facilities and to voluntary patients.

Voluntary Consent to Treatment

Involuntary admission to hospital should be the exception and should happen only in very specific circumstances. The legislation should outline these exceptional circumstances and lay down the procedures to be followed for involuntary admission. The legislation should give patients who are admitted involuntarily the right of appeal against their admission to a review body.

Voluntary treatment is associated with the issue of informed consent. The legislation should ensure that all treatments are

Virginia governor Timothy Kaine signs mental health legislation in 2008. The World Health Organization maintains that mental health legislation must guarantee patient confidentiality.

provided on the basis of free and informed consent except in rare circumstances. Consent cannot be lawful if accompanied by a threat or implied threat of compulsion, or if alternatives to proposed treatment are not offered for consideration.

The legislation should only permit voluntary treatment, i.e. after informed consent has been obtained, of patients admitted voluntarily to mental health facilities. Involuntary patients should also be treated on a voluntary basis except in certain rare situations, e.g. if they lack the capacity to give consent and if treatment is necessary in order to improve mental health and/or prevent a significant deterioration in mental health and/or prevent injury or harm to the patients or other people.

The legislation should lay down procedures for protecting the human rights of people who are being treated involuntarily and should provide them with protection against harm and the misuse of the powers indicated above. These procedures include obtaining an independent second opinion, obtaining permission from an independent authority based on professional recommendations, giving patients access to the right to appeal against involuntary treatment, and using a periodic review mechanism. . . .

The legislation should make provisions for the automatic reviewing of all instances of involuntary admission and involuntary treatment. This should involve an independent review body with legal or quasi-legal status enabling it to act as a regulatory authority. The legislation should specify the composition, powers and duties of such a body.

The legislation should make provision for the appointment of guardians of persons who are not competent to make decisions and manage their own affairs. The procedures for making competence decisions, including the appropriate authority for such decisions and the duties of guardians and protective mechanisms to prevent the abuse of powers by guardians, should be specified in legislation.

Provisions for Other Legislation Impacting Mental Health

The components of legislation concerning sectors outside the health sector are also important for the prevention of mental disorders and the promotion of mental health. Housing is of tre-mendous importance in relation to the integration of persons with mental disorders into communities. Housing legislation should protect the rights of persons with mental disorders, for example by preventing geographical segregation, giving them priority in state housing schemes and mandating local authorities to establish a range of housing facilities.

Children, youth and adults have the right to suitable educational opportunities and facilities. Countries should ensure that the education of people with mental disorders is an integral part of their educational systems. Specific mental health programmes in schools have a role to play in the early identification of emotional and behavioural problems in children and can thus help to prevent disabilities attributable to mental disorders. School-based programmes also help to increase awareness about emotional and behavioural disorders and to develop skills for coping with adversity and stress.

Employment is a key area for the promotion of community integration. The legislation should protect persons with mental disorders from discrimination, exploitation and unfair dismissal from work on grounds of mental disorder. There is also a need for legislation to promote the establishment and funding of vocational rehabilitation programmes, including the provision of preferential financing and affirmative action programmes.

Disability pensions and benefits are another area where legislation can help to protect and promote the rights of persons with mental disorders and further the cause of community integration. Civil legislation should enable persons with mental disorders to exercise all their civil, political, economic, social and cultural rights, including the rights to vote, marry, have children, own property and have freedom of movement and choice of residence. Other areas of legislative action include the improvement of access to psychotropic medication and the provision of mental health services in primary health care.

ELEVEN

A Woman Survives Schizophrenia

Reshma Valliappan

> Reshma Valliappan is associated with the Schizophrenia Awareness Association in India, where she writes and speaks about her experiences with schizophrenia. Valliappan began showing symptoms of schizophrenia when she was twenty-two. She describes her wild behavior, smoking, and hanging out on the streets. Strange thoughts came into her head. She believed her parents were poisoning her, she heard voices, she would sit for hours doing nothing. Once she pulled a knife in her class and threatened her teacher. Valliappan's family watched her vigilantly to prevent her from hurting herself or her friends, but that just made her lose her sense of privacy and independence. She succumbed to living at peace with the people who inhabited her own world in her head. Learning to talk about her illness and realizing that she will always have periods of relapse and recovery have helped her cope with her illness.

About four years ago [ca. 2003], there was a young woman of 22 years of age who smoked a lot, wandered on the street outside her college, drank a lot of alcohol, and did many more dangerous and embarrassing things that didn't embarrass her at that time. This girl had many friends—real friends and unreal

Reshma Valliappan, "Climbing the Mountain," *World Fellowship for Schizophrenia and Allied Disorders Newsletter*, Third Quarter, 2007, pp. 16–17. Reproduced by permission.

friends. But she was caught. Not just in the bad habits that many youngsters like her get caught in, but she was caught in her own mind! The most dangerous obsession started pouring into her life. It ruled her. It ruled everything she did, everything she said, everything she heard-smelled-touched-tasted, and everything she thought. It grew to be more than her thoughts, as she knew others could hear her thoughts.

A Woman Retreats into Her Own Mind

So she stopped thinking.

She stopped talking.

She stopped going out of her house, her room.

All she did was sit idle and talk to herself. She painted once in a while, but smoking filled her daily schedule and she slept most

People who live with schizophrenia often stop talking and are unable to leave the house. They become prisoners in their own minds.

of the time. Eating was a very big decision she had to make as her parents were apparently poisoning her meals. She trusted no one. She was imprisoned in her own mind. Nothing could save her now. Nothing imaginable.

Her parents thought this was the end, and also the beginning of a very sad future they would all have to live with and help her understand. Hope was gone. In fact, her father threw that word out of his dictionary. As for her mother, she hardly even knew that word existed. And her younger sister only lived in confusion.

The dangerous obsession of the young woman grew deeper and stronger over time. Everyone knew something was wrong with her, but didn't have the courage do anything about it.

A couple of weeks passed with many arguments at home about her behaviour. At the same time, her parents were trying not to notice her behaviour. They told themselves it was just a rebellious phase. Then a day came when the young woman stormed into her lecturer's cabin at college and said that she was going to kill every student outside the cabin. Obviously, her lecturer thought she was joking; but then the young woman pulled a knife from her pocket and started talking to herself while walking back and forth. The lecturer closed the door and left her there while she called another colleague for help.

Friends and Family Watch Over Her

What happened after that incident was a one-day roller coaster that went only downwards. Arguments continued at home; the walls felt like prison bars. Fights took place within the young woman. She was suffering, both inside and outside. She looked sick, with dark circles under her eyes, unwashed hair, dirty finger nails and wearing the same set of clothes day after day.

The young woman withdrew from people—her friends, her family, her pet, herself. Days were filled watching TV and interpreting messages from the radio and television. She astral traveled and went to the same place over and over again. Sleeping was no longer an easy thing for her.

Her mother stayed near the bathroom when the young woman bathed, hoping she wouldn't hurt herself. When she wanted cigarettes, her father would walk with her to the shop hoping that she wouldn't run some place else. When she sat in her room doing nothing, her sister would be made to sit in the room too just to make sure she didn't lock the door from inside.

This took away all her privacy. But did that make a difference to her? No. At that point it didn't. Because she didn't know what the word privacy meant anymore. Her life was in danger. People were trying to kill her. Men were tormenting her by calling her names and making her do things she didn't want to do. She knew she was meant for something higher, a great mission she had to accomplish where the whole world depended upon her. This dangerous obsession took her many places she had never been before. Places no one else had even dreamt or imagined could exist and that would lead her to secrets and great power. She called these places "the undiscovered mind."

Relapse and Recovery Is a Part of Life

And this girl is no one else but me.

I couldn't complete my education and had to take a break from everything I once did. It was no more just giving it a go or trying or even struggling. I needed help. The help came in. Family, doctors, counselors, and support groups started making a difference. But somehow with every step forward, a relapse set in and I fell 10 steps behind. Re-starting once again was too much of an effort. Brushing my teeth, taking a bath, grooming myself well, eating and drinking right, I still felt helpless and hopeless. I woke up each morning with suicidal thoughts and slept each night wishing that I would sleep forever because I was useless. I was just a pain to everyone who tried to help me.

As months passed, relapses and recoveries were the only activities in my life. I somehow managed to complete my bachelor's degree and move on to a master's. This has also become another struggle for me as this illness doesn't seem to leave me. No matter what I do, it keeps showing up in a different mask and I have to change the way I look at it. Every time I understand it, there is just more of it to understand. I sometimes feel that I shouldn't have the insight I have. I should just have remained under the

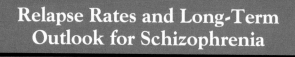

Relapse Rates and Long-Term Outlook for Schizophrenia

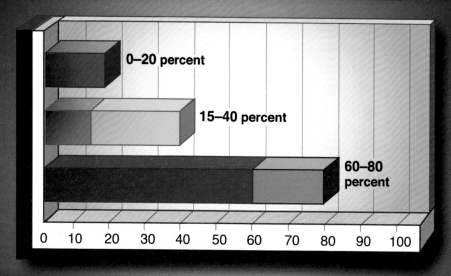

0–20 percent

15–40 percent

60–80 percent

| 0 | 10 | 20 | 30 | 40 | 50 | 60 | 70 | 80 | 90 | 100 |

With medication and adequate psychosocial intervention (family psychoeducation and social skills training)

With medication

Without medication

Taken from: *PRELAPSE*: Preventing Relapse in Schizophrenia.

care of the medications and let them rule my symptoms for me. I do feel sick of it. Sick of the fact that no matter what I do, it is always caused by my symptoms.

I felt there was no me. Who was I? Was I just a combination of all my symptoms? Were they always going to rule what I did and thought? So then I began believing that since I had such an illness, why did I need others to talk to? Doesn't it make sense? I have all those wackos in my head that keep talking to me all the time. They are as real as everyone else. I can touch and feel them too. So why do I need others? Do the real people really matter to me? The answer I gave myself was NO. There was too much of heartache talking to real people; too much hypocrisy in their words and deeds; too much politics and lies. Nothing about these real people and this real world seemed exciting and true. My world was a much safer and nicer place. I didn't have to answer anyone nor hate anyone.

The love among the fellow men in my mind grew. Though I knew I was depending on them I liked it. I felt comfortable. No one would ever be able to take them away from me. But I was not free! I still felt tied down.

She Learns to Talk About Her Illness

It took a lot of time—and effort of my own—to realize this and do something about it. No doctor, medicine, counselor, friend or family could help me with this. I was stuck in my world that I couldn't live without. I felt miserable when the real people were there and miserable when the unreal people were not there. I started living each day with confusion and frustration. I couldn't do anything. How could I chase away the real and call the unreal whenever I wanted to?

A day came when I realized that if I had to live in both these worlds and survive them simultaneously, I had to do something about myself. I obviously couldn't change any of them, though the unreal world was actually a part of me. But I had to look at it as something that was not a part of me to deal with it, because if I did the opposite I would end up living in this unreal world forever and never quite reach anywhere in life. Hence, I decided to speak. Speak to people. The real people. People around me. My parents, sister, friends, everyone. I decided that I had to make a difference in others' lives. I had to move to move others. I had to change for others to change.

As Kahlil Gibran [early twentieth-century Lebanese American poet] said: "And when you have reached the mountain top, then you shall begin to climb." I have always lived by this quote throughout my recovery. I am still recovering and always will be.

TWELVE

A Woman Lives with Bipolar Disorder

British Journal of General Practice

An anonymous general practitioner in Britain describes her descent into rapid cycling bipolar disorder and how it affects her daily life. It began with her feeling irritable with her family, experiencing headaches, and having suicidal thoughts. When her energy levels rise, she feels like mountain biking, driving very fast, or staying up until 3 A.M. When her energy level drops, she becomes irritable, is repelled by the proximity of people, and is hypersensitive to noise. She has tried many treatments, such as antidepressants, mood stabilizers, psychotherapy, and even electroconvulsive therapy. Every day is a struggle as she grasps for a scrap of humanity that remains. Through it all she lost her job and her social life, but thankfully not her family, who have been loyally by her side.

I became unwell suddenly, unexpectedly and severely 5 years ago [in 2001]. I was working as a full-time GP [general practitioner] at the time with a growing [client] list and four small children.

Initially, I had days when I was intensely irritable with my family and suffered from episodes of anxiety and tension headaches. I put these down to the long hours I was working and a full social life at the time. Then driving down the motorway one day

Anonymous, "On Madness: A Personal Account of Rapid Cycling Bipolar Disorder," *British Journal of General Practice*, vol. 56, September 2006, pp. 726–28. Reproduced by permission.

I decided it would be appropriate for me to crash the car and end my life. This was the start of very strong suicidal thoughts and impulses that would pop into my head unbidden and needed real mental energy to resist acting them out.

In the meantime I was also having difficulty working, at times literally dragging a deeply fatigued body and an equally befuddled brain into the consultation, managing by treating one person at a time, rather than look at a whole fully-booked surgery. On other days I found work a useful distractor from the milder symptoms of my depression. Then again, at other times I was full of energy, enjoyed patient contact and was continually looking round for extra things for myself and the family to do.

Rapid Cycling Bipolar Disorder

Gradually, I noticed that working long nights and weekends became intolerable, which I initially put down to having young children rather than believing that I might be ill.

As my mood fluctuated so widely and on a day-to-day basis it was difficult for me to see that I needed help. In the end my husband encouraged me to make an appointment with my GP.

My GP wisely referred me straight on to a psychiatrist. Unwisely she started me on an antidepressant not having asked about symptoms of elevated mood as I was clinically so depressed at the time.

My psychiatrist signed me off work initially with depression, but eventually with bipolar disorder, and thus began several years of treatment.

Antidepressants, mood stabilisers, ECT [electroconvulsive therapy], antipsychotics, thyroid hormones, lithium, psychotherapy and hospital admissions made no difference to the unstable pattern of abrupt mood swings, rapid cycling, bipolar depressions, and mixed mood states with psychotic features woven throughout.

This illness is about being trapped by your own mind and body. It's about loss of control over your life. Bipolar disorder is multipolar, affecting not just energy levels, but behaviour and physiology. To onlookers it seems that your whole personality has changed; the person they know is no longer in evidence. At

Bipolar Mood and Energy Chart

Date:

Medication changes:

Overall mood from 1 (poorest) to 10 (highest) and put into words:

Anxiety:

Irritability:

Depression:

Anger:

Rage:

Distorted thinking:

Hours sleep (night before):

Hours sleep (during day):

Appetite:

Energy level:

Physical problems and symptoms:

External triggers:

Taken from: Patty Fleener, M.S.W. www.mental-health-today.com.

times they can be sucked into believing that the changes are permanent.

My mood may swing from one part of the day to another. I may wake up low at 10 A.M., but be high and excitable by 3 P.M. I may not sleep for more than 2 hours one night, being full of creative energy, but by midday be so fatigued it is an effort to breathe. . . .

I will sometimes drive faster than usual, need less sleep and can concentrate well, making quick and accurate decisions. At these times I can also be sociable, talkative and fun, focused at times, distracted at others. If this state of elevation continues I often find that feelings of violence and irritability towards those I love will start to creep in. Concentration and memory start to wane and I can become hypersensitive to noise. The children making their usual noise and my husband singing can drive me to distraction. . . .

Physical Levels Rise and Fall

Physically my energy levels can seem limitless. The body moves smoothly, there is little or no fatigue. I can go mountain biking all day when I feel like this and if my mood stays elevated not a muscle is sore or stiff the next day. But it doesn't last, my elevated phases are short, mild and generally manageable, but the shift into severe depression or a mixed mood state occurs sometimes within minutes or hours, often within days and will last weeks often without a period of normality. Indeed I often lose track of what normality is.

Initially my thoughts become disjointed and start slithering all over the place. I will feel that I am physically trying to pin them down in my brain, trying to run ideas together in a coherent way. They will sometimes remain rapid and are accompanied by paranoid delusions causing an inner tension that can only be relieved to some extent by physical activity such as pacing a corridor. I start to believe that others are commenting adversely on my appearance or behaviour. I can become very frightened and antisocial. . . .

Physically there is immense fatigue: my muscles scream with pain, an old nephrostomy scar [from kidney surgery] plays up.

I ache down to my bone marrow, my joints feel swollen. I become breathless weeding a small patch of garden and have to stop after 2 minutes. I become clumsy and drop things. The exhaustion becomes so complete that eventually I drop into bed fully clothed. Sometimes I will vomit, my digestive processes halted. I will often sleep without being refreshed for up to 18 hours. At times every muscle in my body will tense up and be totally resistant to relaxation. Sweat will pour off me or I will be caught in an attack of shivering unrelated to the ambient temperature. I will shout over and over again in my mind for help, but never get the words past my lips. . . .

Thoughts of Suicide

I become passionate about one subject only at these times of deep and intense fear, despair and rage: suicide. The suicidal impulses and images can come at any stage of the illness, even in mania, but are at their most intense and irresistible during psychotic phases.

For months at a time I have carried ropes, blades and enough tricyclic antidepressants to kill me twice over, in the boot [trunk] of my car. In the past I have had access to a fatal pharmacoepia of emergency drugs through my general practice work.

I know where to buy a gun. I know the fatal dosages of the drugs I take. I have considered railway crossings, bridges over rivers, driving off roads into valleys and electrocution. I have made close attempts on my life by hanging and drowning over the last few years.

Sadly, the impact of suicide on my children does not avail me when I am ill. I consider myself to be such a huge burden to them at these times that I believe suicide to be a relief, a final gift to them from a mother who can do no more. A person who has reached the limit of endurance. . . .

Fortunately, those who care for me have been able to recognise these unsafe states and admit me to hospital. Then inexplicably, my mood will shift again. . . .

Consequences and Hope

So why am I still here? I don't know. Possibly luck. Possibly the tiny scrap of humanity that remains even in my most psychotic

Living with bipolar disorder is like being trapped by your own mind and body and feeling a loss of control over your life.

and suicidal states, which allows me to express the desperation and loss of control that I am experiencing, so that caregivers and treating clinicians can respond appropriately and keep me safe. A little hope. Some denial.

I have lost my job, intellectual stimulation and my social life. Sometimes I wonder how my marriage holds together and I am continually anxious about the effects of my illness on my children and whether I will end up like too many other people with severe bipolar disorder, separated from them permanently.

There have been relationships broken and distorted, and relationships that have held fast and true through the worst of its manifestations. Making new friends has often been too difficult. Those who know of my illness have sometimes become accommodating and flexible, others have not. . . .

It's taught me that even with the best psychiatric care some people do not respond to medication, do not get better. However, I am grateful that I have had the best care available to me throughout and that I had completed my family before the onset of this illness. I am also grateful that I was able to take out income protection insurance several years prior to becoming ill, otherwise like many other mentally ill people we would be impoverished.

This illness is about having to live life at its extremes of physical and mental endurance, having to go to places that most people never experience, would never want to experience. It has been about having unthought of limitations placed on your life, your career, your family. For my family it's been about adjusting to totally altered dynamics, having a mother who is often unable to be there for them, for them to have to live with the flux of my moods and the disturbance that comes with recurrent hospitalisations.

It's about having to rely on others for help when you are feeling at your most vulnerable and exposed. It's about being stigmatised.

It has become about trying to stay alive and living life fully in the brief periods of normality or mild elevation that occur from time to time.

Otherwise, rapid cycling bipolar disorder is an unrelenting scourge.

What You Should Know About Mental Illness

What Mental Illness Is

- Persistent abnormal behaviors, feelings, or thoughts that impair a person's ability to perform his or her routine, day-to-day tasks.
- The inability to control feelings of hopelessness, anxiety, depression, mania, or fright.
- A consequence of a person's genetic makeup and social environment.
- A range of illnesses that carry a social stigma.

Types of Mental Illness

- Depression: intense feelings of sadness, anxiety, guilt, worthlessness, or hopelessness, accompanied by the physical symptoms of fatigue, insomnia, loss of appetite or overeating, and problems concentrating.
- Bipolar disorder: a form of depression in which a person shifts rapidly from feelings of emotional highs to depressive lows. These intense mood swings between euphoria and hopelessness leave people exhausted and depressed, often susceptible to thoughts of suicide.
- Anxiety disorder: exaggerated feelings of worry, terror, or irritability that can last for months. Symptoms include sleeplessness, feelings of incapacitation, and trembling or twitching.

- Schizophrenia: a brain disease in which a person hears voices or believes that other people are trying to harm him or her. It is characterized by erratic behavior and disorganized speech.
- Panic disorder: the sudden spontaneous feeling of terror and dread that sweeps over a person, usually in public places. This person is worried that he or she has no control over where or when the feelings might happen again.
- Eating disorders: an obsession with food intake and/or evacuation. Anorexia nervosa sufferers obsess about food and limit the amount of calories they consume, believing they are fat no matter how skinny they become. Bulimia nervosa sufferers binge on large meals then purge the food from the body with laxatives or self-induced vomiting.

Facts About Mental Illness
- About 20 percent of Americans will suffer from depression once in their lifetime.
- Two-thirds of Americans suffering from a mental illness do not seek treatment.
- According to the Substance Abuse and Mental Health Services Administration the cost to treat mental illness is $55 billion a year.
- Many people who suffer from mental illness also suffer from drug or alcohol abuse.
- One-third of people who seek care from a general physician are also suffering from a mental illness.
- The cause of schizophrenia has a genetic component. The risk of someone in the general population getting schizophrenia is 1 percent. The risk for the child of a parent who has schizophrenia is 13 percent.
- According to a survey by the National Alliance on Mental Illness, twice as many Americans suffer from schizophrenia than HIV/AIDS.
- Forty percent of the homeless and 20 percent of inmates have mental illnesses.

What You Should Do About Mental Illness

Fight the Stigma

Fear of the stigma of mental illness is the main reason that many afflicted people do not seek treatment. It would mean being isolated and discriminated against for jobs and housing. Even their peers might disrespect or mistrust or be afraid of them.

The stigma stems mainly from society's fear that mentally ill people are also violent people. However, according to *Mental Health: A Report of the Surgeon General*, violent behavior is a characteristic of only a few mental psychoses. "There is very little risk of violence or harm to a stranger from casual contact with an individual who has a mental disorder," the report says.

To help fight this stigma, simply be polite and respectful when you speak about the mentally ill or to them. If you have friends or acquaintances with a mental disorder, assure them of your continued support and friendship. And most important of all, encourage them to seek treatment if they have not already done so.

Seek Treatment

Do not suffer in silence. If you display symptoms of a mental illness yourself, visit a general physician first for a complete diagnosis. Many physical ailments accompany emotional concerns. Once the physician believes you may be suffering from a mental illness, he or she will refer you to a psychiatrist or psychologist. For milder cases of general mental distress, you might visit a school counselor, clergy member, or family therapist to talk about your issues.

Treatment for mental illness varies with the specific disease and the person. Prescription medication includes antidepressants, antipsychotics, and antianxiety medications. Psychotherapy involves cognitive behavior therapy, family or group therapy, hospitalization, and, in extreme cases, electroconvulsive therapy.

When a health care professional prescribes a treatment method for you, follow it precisely. Prescription drugs may have unpleasant side effects, but the medication will be beneficial and relieve your symptoms. If the treatment is counseling, go to all the sessions even if you feel fine or are uncomfortable talking to the counselor.

Practice Prevention and Self-Help

Just as physical diseases might be cured if caught early, mental illness might be prevented or relieved if you pay attention to warning signs. Such signs may include unusual anxiety, trouble concentrating, intense worrying over small issues, hearing voices, difficulty sleeping, or losing your appetite.

Many self-help methods can be used to stay mentally healthy and divert your attention from minor problems in your life:

- Participate in a sport or hobby. Physical and creative activities focus your energy on healthy pursuits.
- Find a support group in your school or community where people share experiences and feelings like yours.
- Avoid drugs and alcohol, which can exacerbate already developing feelings of depression or anxiety.
- Find ways to relieve stress, either through meditation, relaxation techniques, or yoga. Stress relief allows you to put life's problems into context and lets you confront them safely.
- Ask your doctor about talk therapy, which can identify an emerging condition, such as depression.

Volunteer to Help Those with Mental Illness

Take a proactive stand by volunteering in your community. Volunteering provides experience if you are seeking a career in social science or medicine. It also teaches character and responsibility and offers the reward of helping a person in need.

To help your community, you can:
- Participate in fund-raisers, such as walk-a-thons, sales, or conferences.
- Educate the community through an art, music, or a creative writing awareness campaign.
- Volunteer at your local hospital.

Learn About Legislation

Research and learn about the laws concerning mental illness and laws that protect people with mental illness. These laws are always evolving as diseases are better understood and better diagnosed. Earlier laws that focused on managing mental illness are being revised and updated. Today more focus is put on prevention, on promoting recovery, and on allowing mentally ill people to give back to their community and become productive citizens. In 2008, legislation by the U.S. Congress is being debated to force health insurance companies to provide treatment for mental diseases on a par with physical illnesses.

ORGANIZATIONS TO CONTACT

The editors have compiled the following list of organizations concerned with the issues debated in this book. The descriptions are derived from materials provided by the organizations. All have publications or information available for interested readers. The list was compiled on the date of publication of the present volume; the information provided here may change. Be aware that many organizations take several weeks or longer to respond to inquiries, so allow as much time as possible.

American Academy of Child and Adolescent Psychiatry (AACAP)
3615 Wisconsin Ave. NW, Washington, DC 20016-3007
(202) 966-7300
Web site: www.aacap.org

The AACAP is composed of child and adolescent psychiatrists who actively research, evaluate, diagnose, and treat psychiatric disorders.

American Psychiatric Association (APA)
1000 Wilson Blvd., Ste. 1825, Arlington, VA 22209-3901
(703) 907-7300
Web site: www.psych.org • Web site: www.healthyminds.org

The APA is a medical specialty society that works to ensure humane care and effective treatment for all persons with mental disorders. Its Healthy Minds Web site provides information on common mental health concerns, including warning signs of mental disorders, treatment options, and preventative measures.

Anxiety Disorders Association of America (ADAA)
8730 Georgia Ave., Ste. 600, Silver Spring, MD 20901
(240) 485-1001
Web site: www.adaa.org

The ADAA is a nonprofit organization that provides information about anxiety disorders to the public, health care professionals, and legislators. The ADAA promotes the early diagnosis, treatment, and cure of anxiety disorders. ADAA members include clinicians, researchers, and the public.

International Society for Traumatic Stress Studies (ISTSS)
60 Revere Dr., Ste. 500, Northbrook, IL 60062
(847) 480-9028
Web site: www.istss.org

The ISTSS is an international multidisciplinary organization that provides information and conducts research about severe stress and trauma. The group promotes understanding and consequences of traumatic exposure, advocates for traumatic stress research, and supports prevention of traumatic events.

National Alliance on Mental Illness (NAMI)
Colonial Place Three, 2107 Wilson Blvd., Ste. 300
Arlington, VA 22201-3042
(800) 950-6264
Web site: www.nami.org

NAMI is the nation's largest grassroots mental health organization. It is dedicated to improving the lives of persons with mental illness and their families. The organization publishes the magazine *Advocate* as well as an e-newsletter and numerous press releases.

National Institute of Mental Health (NIMH)
6001 Executive Blvd., Rm. 8184, MSC 9663
Bethesda, MD 20892-9663
(866) 615-6464
Web site: www.nimh.nih.gov

NIMH aims to reduce the burden of mental and behavioral disorders through research on the mind, brain, and behavior, and to generate research that will transform prevention of and recovery from mental disorders. NIMH offers free, easy-to-read fact sheets, pamphlets, and booklets that are available in both English and Spanish.

National Mental Health Association (NMHA)
2000 N. Beauregard St., 6th Fl., Alexandria, VA 22311
(800) 969-6642
Web site: www1.nmha.org

The NMHA is the oldest and largest nonprofit organization in the United States that addresses all aspects of mental health and mental illness. NMHA works with more than 340 affiliates to improve the lives of the 54 million Americans with mental disorders through advocacy, education, research, and service.

PsychCentral
Web site: http://psychcentral.com

PsychCentral is an online, independent mental health social network that began as an online support group in 1991. Run by mental health professionals, the site provides information and support communities for people with mental health issues.

Substance Abuse and Mental Health Services Administration (SAMHSA)
U.S. Department of Health and Human Services
PO Box 42557, Washington, DC 20015
(800) 789-2647
Web site: www.mentalhealth.samhsa.gov
Web site: www.allmentalhealth.samhsa.gov

SAMHSA sponsors the National Mental Health Information Center which provides information about mental health via a toll-free telephone number, its Web site, and more than six hundred publications, including the *SAMHSA News*, a quarterly newsletter. The Web site also provides access to the National Library of Medicine and the National Academies Press.

BIBLIOGRAPHY

Books

Xavier Amador, *I Am Not Sick I Don't Need Help.* Peconic, NY: Vida, 2007.

Tracy Anglada, *Intense Minds: Through the Eyes of Young People with Bipolar Disorder.* Victoria, BC: Trafford, 2006.

Charles Barber, *Comfortably Numb: How Psychiatry Is Medicating a Nation.* New York: Pantheon, 2008.

Gerri C. Borenstein, *Therapy.* New York: Scholastic, 2003.

Shirley Brinkerhoff, *Psychiatric Disorders: Drugs and Psychology for the Mind and Body.* Broomall, PA: Mason Crest, 2004.

Bev Cobain, *When Nothing Matters Anymore: A Survival Guide for Depressed Teens.* Minneapolis: Free Spirit, 2007.

James S. Gordon, *Unstuck: Your Guide to the Seven-Stage Journey Out of Depression.* New York: Penguin, 2008.

Robert V. Hine, *Broken Glass: A Family's Journey Through Mental Illness.* Albuquerque: University of New Mexico Press, 2006.

Joseph J. Luciani, *Self-Coaching: The Powerful Program to Beat Anxiety and Depression.* Hoboken, NJ: John Wiley & Sons, 2006.

Richard McLean, *Recovered, Not Cured: A Journey Through Schizophrenia.* Sydney: Allen & Unwin, 2005.

Tracy L. Morris, *Anxiety Disorders in Children and Adolescents.* New York: Guilford, 2004.

Richard O'Connor, *Undoing Depression: What Therapy Doesn't Teach You and Medication Can't Give You.* London: Souvenir, 2007.

Demitri Papolos and Janice Papolos, *The Bipolar Child.* New York: Broadway, 2007.

Elyn R. Saks, *The Center Cannot Hold: My Journey Through Madness.* New York: Hyperion, 2008.

Kurt Snyder, Raquel E. Gur, and Linda Wasmer Andrews, *Me, Myself, and Them: A Firsthand Account of One Young Person's Experience with Schizophrenia.* New York: Oxford University Press USA, 2007.

Claudia J. Strauss and Martha Manning, *Talking to Depression: Simple Ways to Connect When Someone in Your Life Is Depressed.* New York: New American Library Trade, 2004.

Mark G. Williams et al., John D. Teasdale, Zindel V. Segal, and Jon Kabat-Zinn, *The Mindful Way Through Depression: Freeing Yourself from Chronic Unhappiness.* New York: Guilford, 2007.

Periodicals

Joan Archart-Treichel, "Scientists Identify Strategies to Prevent Mental Illness," *Psychiatric News*, May 19, 2006.

Salynn Boyles, "Bipolar Disorder Widely Underdiagnosed," *WebMD Medical News*, May 7, 2007. www.webmd.com.

Mary Carmichael, "Welcome to Max's World," *Newsweek*, May 26, 2008.

Marilyn Elias, "Schizophrenics Battle Stigma, Myths in Addition to Disease," *USA Today*, June 8, 2008.

Terri J. Farmer, "The Experience of Major Depression: Adolescents' Perspectives," *Mental Health Nursing*, September 2002.

Richard A. Friedman, "Violence and Mental Illness—How Strong Is the Link?" *New England Journal of Medicine*, November 16, 2006.

Denise Gellene, "Bipolar Disorder in Youths May Be Over-Diagnosed," *Los Angeles Times*, September 5, 2007.

Daniel Hall-Flavin, "Defining Mental Illness: An Interview with a Mayo Clinic Specialist," CNN.com Health Library, August 17, 2006. www.cnn.com/HEALTH/library/HQ/01079.

Carolyn Y. Johnson, "Doctors See Need for Prevention in Mental Illness," *Boston Globe*, March 1, 2005.

Kathleen Kingsbury, "Talking Out Trauma: Not Always a Help," *Time*, June 5, 2008.

Janet Kornblum, "Families Often 'Lost' in Trauma of Mental Illness," *USA Today*, June 5, 2008.

Julie Rawe, "Children Can Outgrow ADHD," *Time*, November 15, 2007.

Rick Weiss, "Study: U.S. Leads in Mental Illness, Lags in Treatment," *Washington Post*, June 7, 2005.

INDEX

A

Acetylation, of DNA, 33

Adolescents. *See* Youth

Agoraphobia, 12, 23

Akbarian, Schahram, 27

American Journal of Human Genetics, 31

American Psychological Association (APA), 7

Anorexia nervosa, 16

Antidepressants, 32
  increase in use of, 50
  use in adolescents, 66, 69
  use must be monitored to be effective, 65–69

Antipsychotic medication, 9

Anxiety disorders, 11–15, 21

Archimedes, 56

Attention deficit/hyperactivity disorder (ADHD), 13–15
  and bipolar disorder, 61–63, 62

B

BDNF (brain-derived neurotrophic factor) gene, 32

Biochemistry, 25

Bipolar disorder (manic-depressive illness), 15, 23
  epigenetic changes in, 31
  is underdiagnosed in youth, 57–64
  mood/energy chart, 92

personal account of sufferer, 90–96

British Journal of General Practice, 90

Bulimia nervosa, 16–17

C

Character Strengths and Virtues: A Handbook and Classification (Seligman and Peterson), 71–72

Childhood-onset bipolar disorder (COBPD)
  adult-onset vs., 59–60
  attention deficit/hyperactivity disorder and, 61–63, 62
  follow-up studies of, 63

Children. *See* Youth

Chromatin, 31

Clozapine (Clozaril), 9

CpG islands, 29–30

D

Darkness Visible (Styron), 52

Deaths, leading causes of, 78

Depression/depressive disorders, 15–16, 21
  drug treatment of, 9
  genetic aspects of, 32–33
  is overdiagnosed, 48–56
  is underdiagnosed, 41–47
  omega-3 and, 35
  outpatient treatment of, 50

PICTURE CREDITS

Maury Aaseng, 14, 19, 29, 37, 45, 58, 62, 68, 78, 88, 92

© age fotostock/SuperStock, 53, 73

AP Images, 81

© Bubbles Photolibrary/Alamy, 60

© Cristian Baitg Creative Collection/Alamy, 95

Bertrand Demee/Photographer's Choice/Getty Images, 85

Jim Dowdalls/Photo Researchers, Inc., 30

© INSADCO Photography/Alamy, 11

Image copyright Robyn Mackenzie, 2008. Used under license from Shutterstock.com, 35

© PHOTOTAKE Inc./Alamy, 24

Jaye Pratt, 50, 51

© Chris Rout/Alamy, 22

© SuperStock, Inc./SuperStock, 8, 42

© thislife pictures/Alamy, 67